Pointe du Hoc
1944

Battleground Normandy

Pointe du Hoc
1944

Tim Saunders

Pen & Sword
MILITARY

First published in Great Britain in 2018 by
PEN & SWORD MILITARY
An imprint of
Pen & Sword Books Ltd
47 Church Street
Barnsley
South Yorkshire
S70 2AS

Copyright © Tim Saunders, 2018

ISBN 978-1-47388-916-3

A CIP catalogue record for this book is available from the British Library.

Typeset by Concept, Huddersfield, West Yorkshire HD4 5JL.
Printed and bound in England by CPI Group (UK) Ltd, Croydon CR0 4YY.

Pen & Sword Books Ltd incorporates the imprints of Pen & Sword Archaeology,
Atlas, Aviation, Battleground, Discovery, Family History, History, Maritime,
Military, Naval, Politics, Railways, Select, Social History, Transport, True Crime,
and Claymore Press, Frontline Books, Leo Cooper, Praetorian Press,
Remember When, Seaforth Publishing and Wharncliffe.

For a complete list of Pen & Sword titles please contact
PEN & SWORD BOOKS LIMITED
47 Church Street, Barnsley, South Yorkshire, S70 2AS, England
E-mail: enquiries@pen-and-sword.co.uk
Website: www.pen-and-sword.co.uk

Contents

Introduction

The Pointe du Hoe [*sic*] battery was considered the number one priority in the bombardment plan for it was the only enemy position which covered both of the beaches and transport areas.

Admiral Kirk, Commander Western Task Force

If there is any doubt about the priority afforded to the Pointe du Hoc Battery or, as it was known to the D-Day planners, Battery No. 1, Admiral Kirk's post-operational report certainly dispels it. He continues:

Originally there were six 155 mm guns (French type GPF) with an estimated range of 25,000 yards, in open concrete emplacements. It was strategically located atop a 90-foot-high coastal bluff, remote from any large landing beach, surrounded by wire and minefields and extremely well protected on the flanks by prepared strongpoints. Personnel and ammunition shelters

One of the two newly-built but not commissioned casemates showing plenty of battle damage.

were underground and constructed of heavily reinforced mass concrete. Machine gun positions and communication trenches were well dug in and camouflaged.

The action by Colonel James Rudder's 2nd Ranger Battalion, indeed the entire Provisional Ranger Group, in their first battle is without doubt an epic of American military history. The military qualities of ingenuity, the self-confidence of specially-selected and trained troops, determination and fortitude were shown by Colonel Rudder and Colonel Schneider and their men down to the lowest-ranking Ranger.

All of this is self-evident in the story of the preparations for D-Day, scaling the cliffs at the Pointe and at the western end of OMAHA Beach. These achievements alone make a great story, but add in the manner in which Ranger Group C landed on OMAHA and led the way up the bluffs while Rudder's men held out at Pointe du Hoc awaiting relief makes it a truly remarkable story of endeavour.

Those who are not intending to visit Pointe du Hoc may be interested in a companion DVD also available from Pen & Sword.

As ever I am grateful to the Pen & Sword team who have nurtured this book through to publication; in particular Matt Jones who has overseen the process, Pamela Covey who did the editing with remarkable patience and Noel Sadler who designed the book. It is, however, a coincidence that Noel has a personal connection to the events here recounted; his Uncle Bill served as a Royal Navy bowman aboard one of the Ranger's landing craft heading for Dog Green sector of OMAHA beach. He recalled that the Rangers, probably C Company 2nd Battalion, had a substantial fried breakfast, but the long transit in the landing craft through the rough sea made most of them seasick. He also recalled that his landing craft had problems with one of the sandbanks off the beach and had to make several attempts to get over it.

Tim Saunders
Warminster
August 2017

8

Chapter One

Origins of the US Rangers

In American military history, the term 'ranger' was first used in print in the 1750s in *The Boston Weekly News-Letter*:

> All Gentlemen Volunteers and Others that have a mind to serve His Majesty King GEORGE the Second for a limited time in the Independent Companies of Rangers now in Nova Scotia, may apply to Lieutenant Alexander Callender at Mr Jonas Leonard's at the sign of the Lamb at the South End of Boston, where they shall be kindly entertained, enter into present pay, and have good quarters, and when they join their respective companies in Halifax, shall be completely clothed in blue broadcloth, receive arms, accoutrements, provisions and all other things necessary for a gentleman ranger.

The main theatre of war throughout the eighteenth century was Europe, but the likes of the Seven Years' War were effectively world wars that included fighting for control and influence in North America between France and the emerging British Empire, along with their supporters and foes among both settlers and in-digenous peoples. These sub-conflicts are referred to as the French Indian Wars and were distinctly different to the disciplined and formulaic Frederican style of European warfare with its reliance on fire-power and shock tactics.

The 'rangers' are, however, synonymous with the American War of Independence or American Revolutionary War in which the vast, remote and wooded lands of North America contrasted with the more open European countryside and spawned a different style of fighting with the militias (of both sides) being supplemented by irregulars armed with mostly their own musket or the long Pennsylvania rifle. The latter, with its small bore, was a favourite among hunters who were used to taking fleeting shots at their quarry as it minimized damage to furs. Among these semi-irregular forces were His Majesty's Independent Companies of American Rangers. Major Rogers approached the British military authorities with an offer to form a number of companies of backwoodsmen and Indian fighters.

An eighteenth-century ranger. The Queen's Rangers fought for the British during the Revolutionary War.

The Standing Orders that Major Rogers wrote deliberately in common prose for his companies can easily be followed in the ethos of the Rangers some 170 years later:

- Don't forget nothing. Have your musket clean as a whistle, tomahawk scoured, sixty rounds, powder and ball, and be ready to march at a moment's notice. When you are on the march act the way you would if you were sneaking up on a deer, see the enemy first.
- Tell the truth about what you see and what you do. There is an army depending on us for correct information. You can

lie all you please when you tell others about the Rangers, but don't lie to a ranger or an officer.

- Don't never take a chance you don't have to. When on the march single file far enough apart so one shot can't go through two men. If we strike swamps or soft ground, we spread out abreast, so it's hard to track us. When we march we keep moving till dark, so as to give the enemy the least possible chance at us.
- When in camp, half the party stays awake, while the other half sleeps. If we take prisoners, we keep 'em separate till we have time to examine them so they can't cook up a story between them.
- Don't ever march home the same way. Take a different route so you won't be ambushed. Each party has to keep about 20 yards ahead, 20 yards on each flank and 20 yards in the rear so the main body can't be wiped out. Every night you will be told where to meet if surrounded by a superior force.
- Don't sit down without posting sentries.
- Don't sleep beyond dawn; dawn's when the French and Indians attack.
- Don't cross the river by the regular ford. If somebody is trailing you make a circle, come back on your own tracks and ambush the folks that's aiming to ambush you.
- Don't stand up when the enemy is aiming at you; kneel down, lie down or hide behind a tree. Let the enemy come till he's almost close enough to touch, then let him have it and jump up and finish him off with your tomahawk.

Outbreak of the Second World War

The United States joined the allies in the First World War as a response to unrestricted German submarine warfare, rapidly expanding her army and suffering more than 300,000 casualties on the Western Front. In the aftermath of the war, however, with isolationism and a lack of credible military threat to her borders the US army shrank rapidly. In the foreword to the army chief of staff's post-war report describing the state of the US army in July 1939, a staff officer wrote:

For the feat of transforming the miniscule interwar Army to the great force that defeated the Axis in Africa, Europe, the

Pacific, and Asia, no one could claim more credit than [General George C.] Marshall. When he took office, the 174,000-man U.S. Army ranked nineteenth in size in the world, behind Portugal and only slightly ahead of Bulgaria. Its half-strength divisions were scattered among numerous posts, its equipment obsolete, its reliance on the horse increasingly anachronistic.

US industry rose to the matériel challenge of not only supplying Britain but designing and manufacturing a whole new range of equipment for the US army in a very short time, based largely on commonality of parts. In an army that rapidly burgeoned to 8.3 million men by the end of the war from fewer than 100,000 pre-war active duty soldiers and an underfunded National Guard, military knowledge and experience was inevitably thinly spread in 1942. In addition, General Marshall was only too aware that this was a war of mobility that was very different from the positional warfare of 1917–18. Pamphlets based on British experience helped but what was needed was knowledge and practical experience on which to base the training of that rapidly-expanding US army.

Colonel Lucian Truscott, shortly to be brigadier general, was instrumental in developing the Rangers based on the British Commandos. In May 1942, he was assigned to the Allied Combined

US troops instructing British tank crewmen on a Lend-Lease Lee/Grant tank in the Western Desert.

THE GERMAN SQUAD IN COMBAT . . .

PREPARED BY
MILITARY INTELLIGENCE SERVICE
WAR DEPARTMENT

III

The cover of an early-war US pamphlet based on British experience.

Operations Staff under Lord Mountbatten. Here at the heart of the planning for taking the battle to the enemy Truscott believed that some of the necessary knowledge and experience could be gained during the growing number of increasingly large raids on enemy-held territory alongside British Commandos. As a well-respected officer, Truscott applied to Washington and received permission to raise an American Commando-type unit.

With events moving fast, on 1 June 1942 Colonel Truscott drafted a letter of instructions for Major General Chaney, then commander of US Army Forces British Isles, to sign. It directed Major General Hartle, commanding V US Corps and the American forces in Northern Ireland, to organize the new unit as quickly as practicable. The letter gave guidance for the organization of an American 'commando unit for training and demonstration purposes, which was to be the first step in a program specifically directed by the Chief of Staff for giving actual battle experience to the maximum number of personnel of the American Army.'

Colonel Lucian Truscott photographed between the two world wars.

Combined Operations badge.

The name 'commando', however, was too typically British for American taste, being redolent of the disliked Empire, so the US army looked back into their own military traditions and came up with the name Rangers; a name that encapsulated the American backwoodsmen's tactics used by irregular units during the wars of the eighteenth century. More than that, the very word 'ranger' perfectly summed up the Commando ethos required of an American soldier in a way that needed little explanation to the average GI. Just in case anyone was in doubt, Major Rogers' orders dating back to the Revolutionary Wars formed the basis of what is with some modifications today still the essence of the Ranger Creed.

There is still some debate as to whether it was intended to raise an American 'Commando' unit as a permanent part of the US order of battle in the European theatre or, as many consider, the unit was to be a temporary expedient to gather that knowledge and experience, i.e. for 'demonstration purposes'.

In the early summer of 1942 the first US troops starting to arrive in the United Kingdom's province of Northern Ireland found themselves in what was essentially a military backwater with little of the army training activity with armoured forces, etc. that was under way in mainland Britain. Consequently, the 34th Red Bull Infantry Division (activated National Guard from the mid-west states) provided most of the volunteers from which the US troops in Northern Ireland would revive a great American military tradition and form the new generation of US Rangers. Other American units also contributed volunteers including Captain William O'Darby, a bored V US Corps Headquarters officer thirsting for action.

How O'Darby became the first Ranger commanding officer reflects a similarity with the British Commandos: being in the right place at the right time and grasping an opportunity! On the first Sunday in June Major General Hartle was on his way to church in Belfast accompanied by the chief of staff and en route discussed the need to find a first-rate officer to command the new battalion. The general's aide-de-camp, artillery Captain O'Darby, was immediately suggested and readily agreed to the assignment and went on to become one of the most successful US combat officers of the war.

The 1st US Ranger Battalion started to form in the town of Carrickfergus, with rapidly-promoted Major O'Darby in charge. Working to General Chaney's instructions, Major O'Darby set

Major William O'Darby: the first Ranger commander of the modern era.

about interviewing more than 1,000 volunteers. He would only consider

> fully trained soldiers of the best type [who] were to be sought, and officers and NCOs were to have superior leadership qualities with special emphasis placed upon initiative, sound judgment, and common sense. All men were to have a high level of physical stamina, have natural athletic ability, and be without physical defects.

While no age limit was prescribed for US Ranger candidates, it was pointed out that British Commandos had an average age of 25 and men joining the Ranger Battalion had to be capable of the same exertion and endurance expected of their British counterparts. In addition,

> military and civilian skills, such as self-defence, marksman-ship, scouting, mountaineering, seamanship, small boat

handling and demolition are especially desirable. Men who are familiar with railway engines, power plants and radio stations and who know how to destroy them most effectively on raids are also to be sought.

The first task was to select officers, and these included Max Schneider who subsequently commanded the 5th Rangers on D-Day. Among those recruited were the essential specialists such as medical and communications officers. This was followed on 11 June by interviews of the 700 enlisted men who had volunteered as a result of a cryptically-worded appeal. During a ten-day period in early June 1942, the number of candidates found to be suitable by the officer interview boards and who passed the enhanced medical examination was whittled down to 575. Taking into account a projected failure and injury rate, Major O'Darby's officers were dispatched on further recruiting drives around units in Northern Ireland:

The 1st Ranger Battalion was officially activated on 19 June 1942 and the candidates were immediately into ten days of preliminary 'beat-up', predominantly physical training in Northern Ireland. On 28 June, the Rangers shipped across from Larne to Scotland and the Commando Depot at Achnacarry. Here they undertook the standard commando course undertaken by British Royal Marines and Army candidates, run by the renowned trainer Lieutenant Colonel Vaughn and his British staff. The emphasis was on physical robustness, agility of mind and body along with realistic tactical exercises. These involved the full range of commando environments such as cliff-climbing, boat-handling and speed marches with all exercises containing a high proportion of live ammunition. There were the usual casualties including three Ranger candidates wounded during the live firing exercises.

The majority of Major O'Darby's Rangers qualified for the coveted green beret of the British Commando and the dagger by the end of July. The beret was, of course, not adopted by the Rangers but the Commando dagger was. At this point the yellow and blue Ranger diamond and tabs still lay in the future. These distinctions of dress, so common later in the war, had not yet been authorized.

On 1 August, most of the 1st Ranger Battalion moved to Inveraray on the west coast of Scotland where they undertook four

The Commando dagger – also carried by the US Rangers.

weeks of continuation training and exercises in the form of amphibious training with the Royal Navy using the latest assault landing craft.

Being very much modelled on and initially expected to work alongside the British Commandos, it is no surprise that to start with the Ranger organization closely reflected that of its British counterpart. There were, however, some differences from the outset, particularly with weapons and equipment in which American equivalents of British weapons were used, for instance with the American 60mm mortar being substituted for the Commandos' 2-inch. At this stage the Rangers serving in the European theatre

British Commando Lord Lovat with the first batch of US Rangers, summer 1942.

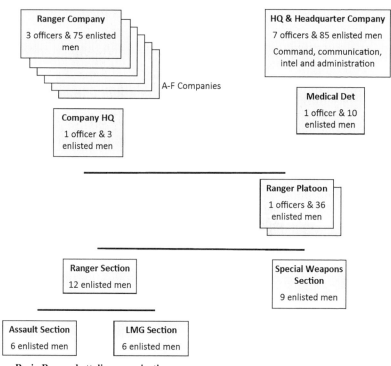

Basic Ranger battalion organization.

were essentially amphibious raiders and only had the same limited, almost theoretical, parachute capability as their British counterparts.

At this stage the 1st US Ranger Battalion came under the Commando Group for operational tasking but remained under the command of the 34th US Infantry Division for administration and logistics.

Operation JUBILEE: The Dieppe Raid

Almost immediately on completion of the Commando course, in pursuit of their task to gain practical combat experience, five officers and forty-six Rangers were sent to join British and Canadian forces preparing for a significant operation. Brigadier Truscott had been made aware of the on/off Operation JUBILEE,

The 1st Rangers boat training at Achnacarry in Scotland.

the proposed raid on the port of Dieppe on the north coast of France.

Following the costly success of the Saint-Nazaire raid, Headquarters Combined Operations had been planning a raid on an altogether different scale involving three Commando units and the best part of 6,000 infantry from the 2nd Canadian Infantry Division. In the British Official History 'Grand Strategy' series is a record of the meeting held in the White House on 9 June 1942: 'Mr Roosevelt had stressed the great need for American soldiers to be given the opportunity of fighting [in the west] as soon as possible.'

President Roosevelt.

Also, having been persuaded to adopt the Germany-first policy by Churchill, the public relations advantage of Americans being seen to be fighting the Germans at this early stage in the war was not lost on President Roosevelt.

19

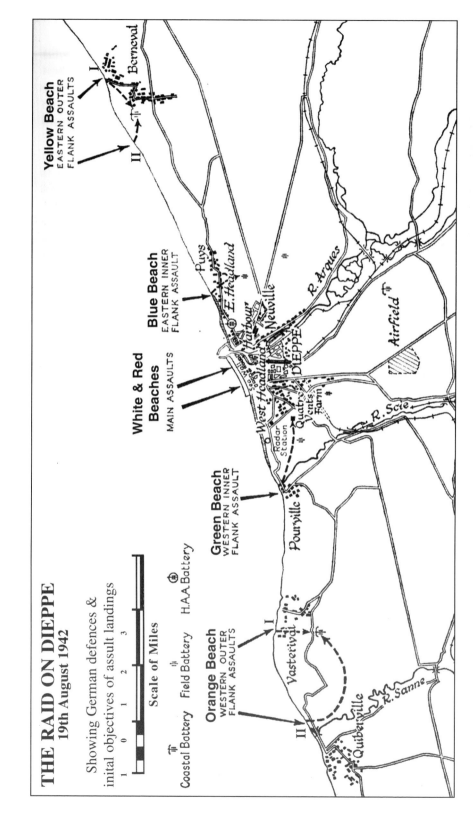

THE RAID ON DIEPPE
19th August 1942

Showing German defences &
inital objectives of assult landings

Scale of Miles

Coastal Battery   Field Battery   H.A.A Battery

Yellow Beach
EASTERN OUTER
FLANK ASSAULTS

Berneval

Blue Beach
EASTERN INNER
FLANK ASSAULT

Puys

E. Headland

Neuville

Harbour

White & Red Beaches
MAIN ASSAULTS

DIEPPE

West Headland

Quatre Vents Farm

Radar Station

R. Arques

Airfield

R. Scie

Green Beach
WESTERN INNER
FLANK ASSAULT

Pourville

Orange Beach
WESTERN OUTER
FLANK ASSAULTS

Vasterival

Quiberville

R. Sanne

The bloody aftermath of the Dieppe raid.

Consequently, the Rangers were distributed among both Commando and Canadian infantry units in order to gain as wide a cross-section of experience as possible. The resulting action on 19 August is considered to be the first involvement of US soldiers in combat and fighting alongside the British and Canadians, in which they suffered their first casualties from enemy action. The cost to the Rangers was two officers and four Rangers killed in action, with four men being among those captured during the chaos of the withdrawal. Brigadier Truscott and the now Lieutenant Colonel O'Darby had much to think about!

With US military power expanding exponentially, the Dieppe raid was the only operation in which members of the 1st Rangers fought 'under instruction' of the British. With Operation TORCH – the Allied invasion of North Africa – being planned and involving several corps of American troops, there was no longer a need for the Rangers to take part in British operations to gain knowledge and experience.

The Rangers left Scotland in shipping of Force O, a part of the Central Task Force heading to attack the Algerian port of Oran. The attack by the 1st Ranger Battalion on the Vichy French Arzew coastal gun battery was immediately successful and proved to be one of the few well-executed parts of operations to capture Oran.

The 1st Ranger Battalion capturing a French coastal battery at Arzew, east of Oran, December 1942.

Ranger training in North Africa, early 1943.

As a result of the impressive performance during Operation TORCH, the 1st Rangers provided cadres to form the 3rd and 4th Ranger battalions. The three battalions would operate as a Ranger Group during operations in the Mediterranean.

Rudder's Rangers

Meanwhile, another cadre had already been sent back to the United States to train and form the nucleus of the 2nd US Ranger Battalion. On 1 April 1943, following the selection of nearly 600 men primarily from the 29th, 76th and 80th divisions, the battalion was activated at 'Tent City' Camp Forrest, Tennessee under the command of Lieutenant Colonel Saffarans. As, however, with the 1st Rangers' selection process, men came from other parts of the army including the Air Corps to join the new battalion. In the case of the 2nd Rangers, almost half the candidates were returned to their units as a result of the intensity of the physical and military training.

The basis of Ranger physical fitness was a 5-mile march in one hour, a 9-mile march in two hours and a 25-mile speed march. All these tests were to be completed with weapons, equipment and various weights. A unit history stated: 'If a man fell out on a hike, he would be considered physically unfit for Ranger service and would be transferred from the organization.'

Captain Ralph Goranson of Company C commented on this period of the 2nd Rangers' development:

> To get into the Rangers, you had to volunteer. At any time during training, you could volunteer out because of physical requirements, mental requirement, or just the fact that you just didn't fit. We had a high turnover at the beginning, but as we got ready to leave in early September of '43, we had a pretty crew put together in each of our Ranger companies.

Major James E. Rudder took over command of the 2nd Rangers on 30 June 1943 with a battalion only partly formed and with the formation of a 5th Battalion taking a further cadre of trained men from his unit. Consequently, additional volunteers were called from the 79th, 100th and 106th US Infantry divisions to bring the 2nd Battalion up to strength and to form the 5th. All this required Major Rudder to reorganize his battalion and in the process continue to return to unit those who were not up to his exacting standards of military competence and discipline. Under his command there was a distinct increase in the tempo of physical training and a move from 'Tent City' into barracks at Camp Forrest.

In early September the 2nd Battalion, now physically fit and Ranger-qualified, started a programme of continuation training, first moving to Fort Pierce in Florida for a two-week amphibious assault training package, which was followed in mid-September by another move north to Fort Dix in New Jersey. Here the Rangers were put through an intense small-arms training course focusing

Major James Earl Rudder, a reserve officer activated in 1941 who gained rapid promotion and notice thanks to his military ability.

on and then cross-training on heavier weapons including machine guns, the bazooka and mortars. With the expectation that as a last resort Hitler would use chemical weapons, training in the use of gas masks and fighting while wearing them was undertaken.

Finally, with the build-up for the Cross-Channel attack and D-Day well under way, the 2nd Ranger Battalion boarded the crowded British liner *Queen Elizabeth* in New York on 11 November 1943. Stripped of her comforts, she was bound for the Scottish port of Greenock. A long, cold and slow train journey south then followed to Bude on the north coast of Cornwall.

Ranger Owen Brown describes what was waiting for them:

We arrived at Bude, Cornwall on December 2, 1943. 500 rangers were greeted with 500 pairs of boxing gloves and a few miles of rope for our training on the cliffs of Cornwall. We climbed the cliffs along the Cornish coast and hiked the hills inland, just for conditioning.

At Bude, in common with British Commando practice, the Rangers were billeted four to a civilian house rather than barracks, which of course required self-discipline and planning to be on parade at the right time with the right kit. Even though Rangers were only based at Bude for three weeks, it was a memorable and gentle introduction to the 'Brits' but sadly most of the 'belles of the town' had already been secured by American artillerymen who had been in camps nearby for some time.

In wintry conditions, on the sheer cliffs of Devon and Cornwall, many with narrow tidal beaches, the Rangers were trained in the art of scaling cliffs under the instruction of Commandos.

The presence of the Rangers in Bude in what would otherwise have been another austere, heavily-rationed wartime Christmas for the local people was a bonus. The Rangers, who were ordered to spend the festive season in the town rather than London, supplemented their host family's meagre rations and shared the bounty of items available from the Post Exchange (PX, the US military equivalent of the NAAFI) that many civilians had not seen for several years.

After their first Christmas away from home, the Rangers moved to billets in Titchfield and the surrounding villages in Hampshire, conveniently close to HMS *Tormentor* at Warsash, from where the Commando Group's landing craft operated. Rumours were soon circulating that this was planned in order that they could take part in raids on the enemy-held coast. Indeed, such a raid was in preparation with Calais being the objective for two Ranger companies in late January, but due to heavy seas the raid was cancelled, much to the frustration of the ninety-four Rangers who had been training hard for the mission. Another raid on the Channel Island of Herm was similarly called off, with frustration mounting.

Training continued with the emphasis on amphibious landings, attack and reconnaissance tasks once ashore and in early February the Rangers moved to the Isle of Wight to incorporate climbing the chalk cliffs of Freshwater Bay in their training.

Major Max Schneider.

Meanwhile, the 5th Ranger Battalion, after struggling to find men of sufficient quality, was activated on 1 September 1943 at Camp Forrest under the command of Major Carter. Following a very similar package of training to the 2nd Battalion they followed the 2nd Rangers to England, where Major Max Schneider took command. He had been executive officer (second-in-command) of the 4th Rangers in Sicily and Italy where the battalion suffered very heavy casualties in the Battle of Cisterna, a failed attempt to break out of the Anzio beachhead. The 4th Battalion was disbanded and, consequently, Schneider was available for reassignment, bringing vital combat experience to the Ranger Force in North-West Europe.

Chapter Two

The German Defenders of Normandy

At the time of planning and assembling intelligence, what was to become V US Corps' sector of Normandy coast between Port en Bessin in the east and the River Taute near Carentan in the west was relatively lightly defended. *Generalleutnant* Wilhelm Richter's lower establishment 716th Coastal Infantry Division held a very long stretch of coast known as Sector H, which stretched some 70 miles from the River Taute to the 7th/15th Army boundary on the River Dives.

As a coastal division, the 716th had just two infantry regiments each of just two battalions and, not only that, the quality of the soldiers was poor. Many of the men and youths were of a lower physical grade; men who earlier in the war would have been excluded from service. Post-Stalingrad and 'Tunisgrad' manpower in the Third Reich was at a premium, so much so that many soldiers who had been wounded or frostbitten were also considered fit enough to man static positions and then there was the practice of using soldiers from the east in German units. Least worrying for the commanders were the *Beute Deutsch* (literally 'boot Germans'), soldiers from the annexed territories such as Poland, who reluctantly found themselves to be Germans and, therefore, subject to

Generalleutnant **Wilhelm Richter, commander of the 716th Coastal Infantry Division.**

conscription like every other citizen of the Reich. Of much greater concern was the employment of former Soviet prisoners of war who had found themselves coerced, as a result of the dreadful camp conditions, to 'volunteer' to serve in the Wehrmacht. Not unnaturally, these German-officered *Ost-Bataillone*, of which there were at least three in the invasion area, were unreliable, including 439th *Ost-Bataillone* in the OMAHA area.

Osttruppen **(eastern troops) battalions made up of former Red Army soldiers principally from the Soviet republics.**

Like many formations in the west, the 716th Division was equipped with a mix of vehicles such as captured military or even requisitioned civilian trucks and cars. The majority of the division's logistic tail, in common with 80 per cent of the German army, remained horse-drawn thanks to the lack of preparation in depth for a war that Hitler's adventurism had started prematurely in 1939. The Führer had committed the Wehrmacht to a struggle four years before – in his own estimation – they would be ready for renewed war.

Vehicles were not the only area in which substitution for German weapons and equipment was made. A mix of small arms, principally captured Russian, was to be found across the division, along with French, Czechoslovakian and Russian artillery pieces. What coastal divisions lacked in infantry they made up for with a generous allocation of this artillery but, crucially, the guns had few vehicles or horses with which to redeploy them once battle had been joined.

The Atlantic Wall

The Germans had been steadily increasing their defences all along the coast since the early days of the occupation in 1940 but it had been a low priority, well behind supplying those fighting on the Eastern Front. This remained the case until the autumn of 1943 when the inevitability of an Allied invasion brought a new urgency to the construction of the Atlantic Wall. Consequently Hitler, now unable to avoid committing resources in the west, issued Führer Directive 51 in late 1943:

> All signs point to an offensive on the Western Front no later than spring, and perhaps earlier.
>
> For that reason, I can no longer justify the further weakening of the West in favour of other theatres of war. I have therefore decided to strengthen the defences in the West, particularly at places where we shall launch our long-range [V-weapon] war against England. For those are the very points at which the enemy must and will attack: there – unless all indications are misleading – the decisive invasion battle will be fought.

The drive to the now priority defensive measures was given by the appointment of Rommel to the command of Army Group B in northern France and up the Channel coast to Holland. His appointment was, however, a double one, as he was also inspector of the Atlantic Wall, which stretched from Denmark to the Pyrenees Mountains.

With incredible vigour, Rommel set about constructing what he described as a 'devil's garden' of obstacles. He drove his soldiers and workers hard and in many places, despite supply difficulties, they worked shifts covering twenty-four hours. In six months, they laid the majority of the 1.2 million tons of steel and poured 17.3 million cubic yards of concrete used in the construction of Festung Europa (Fortress Europe). This labour and resources produced a crust of mutually-supporting defended localities. All along the coast, these *Widerstandsnest* (resistance nests) and their larger cousins *Stützpunkt* (strongpoints) were surrounded by more than 4 million anti-tank and anti-personnel mines (many recycled

Feldmarschall **Erwin Rommel, with General Erich Marks, commander of LXXXIV Corps, to his left.**

from the Maginot and Sudeten defences), while on the beaches 500,000 obstacles of various types were constructed.

German Defensive Strategy in the West

Having been in Italy at the time of the Salerno landings and seen how General Mark Clark's Anglo-American Fifth US Army was nearly thrown back into the sea by a panzer division that was immediately inland from the beaches, Rommel believed that these were the tactics that he must adopt. This was backed up by his experience of feeling the lash of Allied fighter-bombers in North Africa and on the basis of these arguments he insisted that Panzer Group West with the bulk of the German armour in France and Belgium would with an even less favourable air situation be lucky to reach the beaches, let alone do so in a timely manner. By this time Allied fighter-bombers with an extended operational capability were ranging across northern France and would with the invasion surely interdict the panzer divisions on their march to the coast.

Seasoned panzer commanders, however, pointed out that the battles on the Salerno Plain, well in range of Allied naval gunfire,

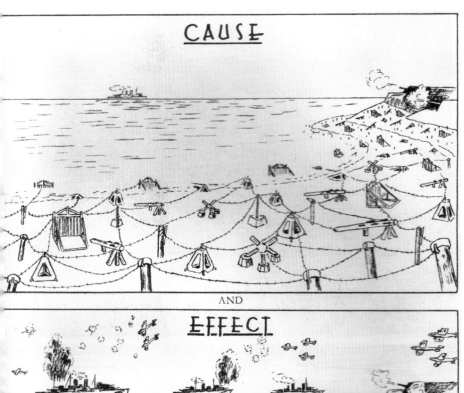

The 'devil's garden' – cause and effect – with which Rommel sought to confront the Allies.

were fought at a considerable cost in knocked-out armoured fighting vehicles (AFVs). They argued that the conventional strategy of letting the enemy commit himself and then concentrating to drive him back into the sea would be most appropriate.

At the time of the invasion neither strategy had been fully adopted. Hitler compromised and gave Rommel some panzers but not enough to implement his 'string of pearls' strategy; i.e. tanks positioned at vulnerable spots capable of intervening in the battle for the beaches.

Despite the compromise that saw some armour being brought forward to within 5 to 10 miles of the coast, the hedgerow country inland of the western part of Sector H, the future OMAHA area, was inherently unsuitable for armoured warfare. The area where V US Corps was to land was therefore a low priority for deployment of such panzers as were available and only a single *Sturm-geschütz* (assault gun, abbreviated to StuG) battalion was capable of being deployed to the OMAHA/Pointe du Hoc area on D-Day.

Reinforcement of Sector H

According to Rommel, Hitler insisted that 'The enemy's entire landing operation must under no circumstances be allowed to last longer than a matter of hours or, at the most, days. Once the landing has been defeated it will under no circumstances be repeated.'

Without panzers to form his 'string of pearls', Rommel argued that in the western part of Coastal Defence Sector H, the number of troops needed to be increased significantly. Consequently, the sector was divided into two, with the 716th Coastal Infantry Division retaining responsibility for the defences east of Port en Bessin, while the 352nd Infantry Division was ordered forward from the St Lo area where it had been formed and was training.

The 352nd was a relatively newly-raised, field-grade division that had been destined to fight on the Eastern Front once fully manned, trained and equipped. Its soldiers were of a distinctly better quality than those found in the coastal divisions and its officers and NCOs were experienced commanders. The 2nd and 5th Rangers would find this very much the case as they respectively struggled to hold and relieve Pointe du Hoc.

Oberstleutnant Ziegelmann, 352nd's chief of staff, having been sent forward to inspect Sector H1 found that only 45 per cent of the bunkers could withstand artillery fire and 15 per cent air attack and that much of the Atlantic Wall was still non-existent. Ziegelmann, however, several months later reported to *Generalleutnant* Kraiss:

1. The 352nd is prepared for combat actions in either offensive or defensive roles.

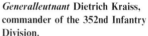

Generalleutnant Dietrich Kraiss, commander of the 352nd Infantry Division.

Generalleutnant Marks, commander of LXXXIV Corps.

2. The battle area assigned to the 352nd, both coastal and inland, has been greatly improved despite all the persistent problems.

3. The individual and small unit training has progressed well with all of the units rating a combat-effective status far above the other units in the area. However, the goals set by *Generalleutnant* Kraiss have not been reached as yet.

The chief of staff made it clear in his report that overall Sector H1 was not ready to withstand a major Allied assault. This was echoed by *Generalleutnant* Kraiss in his reports to *Generalleutnant* Marks at LXXXIV Corps HQ.

The new defensive layout was as follows. The in-place infantry companies of the 716th Division, 726 *Infanterie-Regiment*, were to remain in their defensive position coming under command of the 352nd's 916th *Grenadier-Regiment* whose battalions would be responsible for the sector from Colleville-sur-Mer to Grandcamp.

On D-Day, 914 *Infanterie-Regiment* with 439 *Ost-Bataillone* under command was responsible for the sector from the River Taute in the Carentan area east to Grandcamp-Maisy. *Oberst* Walter Korfes' regimental headquarters of 726 *Infanterie-Regiment* took command of the less vulnerable clifftop positions east of OMAHA to Port en Bessin. Two battalions of 915 *Infanterie-Regiment* were located at Bayeux as LXXXIV Corps reserve, with the 352nd Fusilier Battalion mounted on a mix of bicycles and French trucks.

Largely because the companies of 726 *Infanterie-Regiment* remained in place amid the construction activity all along the coast, the arrival of this new division went unnoticed, unlike the deployment of the 91st *Luftlande-Division* on the Cotentin Peninsula, which was spotted in early May. Consequent adjustments were hastily made to the plan for the two American airborne divisions. The 352nd Division was, however, only detected in the final days before D-Day. The 21st Army Group's Intelligence Summary issued on 5 June 1944 obliquely stated 'It would not be a surprise to find that 352nd Infantry Division had moved forward to the coast.'

Superimposed on the defences were the coastal batteries, which had been *Kriegsmarine* (Nazi German navy) but most of which had been transferred to the army and re-numbered. The German naval strategy for the Normandy coast concentrated on defending the ports and the mouth of the River Seine; consequently there were only two batteries specifically tasked and sited to engage shipping in what was to become V US Corps' area: those at Longues-sur-Mer (see *Battleground* Gold Beach – Jig Green) and the six 155mm guns at Pointe du Hoc.

See map on p. 36

The Pointe du Hoc Battery

The Pointe du Hoc Battery, for much of its existence known to the Germans as the *Cricqueville-en-Bessin Batterie*, had been established early in the occupation on the triangular headland of Pointe du Hoc. The site offered commanding views out to sea from its elevated position on 100ft-high cliffs from where German gunners, in accordance with the naval practice of being able to see targets out to sea, could use a combination of observed and direct fire against shipping.

The guns at Pointe du Hoc were First World War 155mm-calibre weapons but the exact type and mix issued to the 2nd Battery, 832nd Coastal Artillery Battalion is a matter of some debate. The two candidates are the modified *Canon de 155 L modèle 1916*

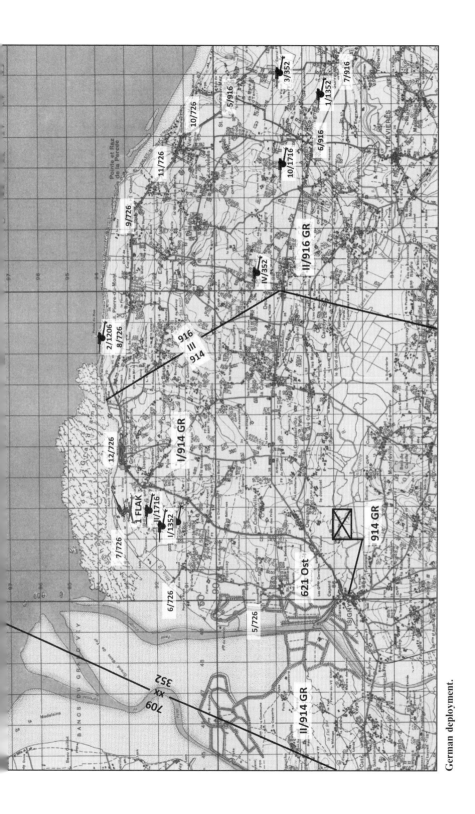

German deployment.

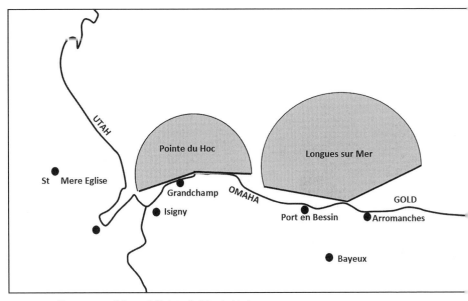

Longues-sur-Mer and Pointe du Hoc batteries.

St. Chamond and *Canon de 155 GPF modèle 1917*, both captured in quantity during 1940 and designated by the Germans, with some modifications, as the 15.5cm K420[f] and the 15.5cm K418[f] respectively. These 155mm guns had a range of between 9.5 and 12 miles with the type and quality of ammunition available in mid-1944. The minimum range was believed to be just under a mile.

This, analysts believed, would enable the battery to engage shipping on the approaches to what were to become OMAHA and UTAH beaches. Pointe du Hoc was clearly a dangerous enemy battery that could imperil the landings.

Initially the guns were dug into revetted earth gun-pits but in 1942 they were replaced by open concrete gun-pits with troops and ammunition shelters. However, German experience of using such open pits during the Salerno landings in Italy during September 1943 convinced them that the guns of key artillery emplacements needed to be casemated if they were to survive in the face of enemy air attack and naval gunfire. Consequently, in late 1943 the decision was made to expand the battery position into a *Stützpunkt*, designated as *Stützpunkt* 75 (S-75). In addition to casemating the guns, the ground defences were enhanced, fields of fire were cleared, ground defences increased and troop shelters built to accommodate the 125 men of the 3rd *Kompanie* 726 *Infanterie-Regiment* in addition to the battery's eighty-five gunners.

One of the Pointe du Hoc guns.

The gun casemates were to be Type 671 and the battery command post (CP) built into the Pointe was Type 636. These standard designs were of course adapted to take into account the site, availability of materials and the whims of engineers, battery and company commanders. Consequently, the near-finished product was far from 'standard'.

In December 1943, the artillery unit at the Pointe du Hoc Battery was redesignated as the 2nd Battery, 1260th Coastal Artillery Battalion.

The type of gun issued to the battery was on D-Day in the process of being changed to one more suitable for firing from the

A Pointe du Hoc gun in an original open gun-pit.

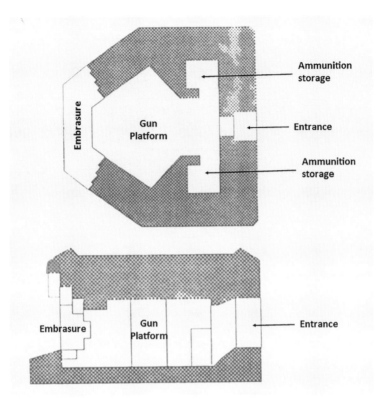

Type 671 gun casemate plan.

confined space of a casemate. The Task Force 122 report, however, states that 'it was learned from prisoners that it was the enemy's intention to install new guns, which were momentarily expected.' Given that the prisoners were predominantly infantrymen, not the gunners, it is entirely possible that this process had already begun.

With work on the first two casemates under way the respective concrete gun-pits were abandoned as shown in the monograph See map on p. 40 and Operational Orders based on air photography. With the development of the battery it is presumed that the rest were sequentially moved to the alternative revetted field positions 1,000 yards to the rear, on the reverse slope beyond the D514 coastal road. The hedges and orchards in that area provided plenty of cover from air photography but the presence of troops, probably the displaced gun crews, in a nearby farm is clearly marked on the Defences

38

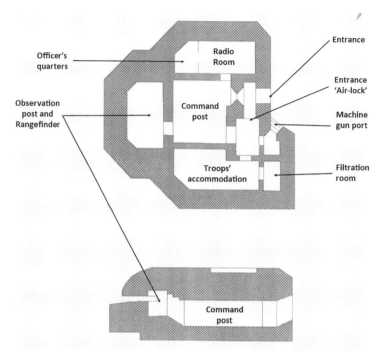

Officer's quarters

Radio Room

Entrance

Entrance 'Air-lock'

Observation post and Rangefinder

Command post

Machine gun port

Troops' accommodation

Filtration room

Command post

Type 636 command post plan.

Overprint map from April onwards in Au Guay and La Montagne farm. It follows that when construction began on the second pair of casemates, the guns would have been similarly moved, leaving just two guns in position on the main battery site. See pp. 46 and 47

The Rangers' intelligence was later able to confirm from captured documents that Nos 1 and 6 guns to the east and west of the battery were to remain in open emplacements with an all-round arc of fire. Guns 2 and 3 were to be in casemates facing OMAHA to the east and guns 4 and 5 were waiting to be installed in casemates facing UTAH. The guns, once casemated, would be restricted to a 120-degree traverse.

With the Allies increasingly dominating the skies, a trio of anti-aircraft casemates was a priority. This was of course important to any fixed fortification in Normandy as signs of construction were very obvious. In the case of Pointe du Hoc, defence against aircraft attacking from up to medium altitude was provided by 20mm anti-aircraft guns sited to the east and west of the gun-pits. Against

LAYOUT OF TYPICAL BATTERY

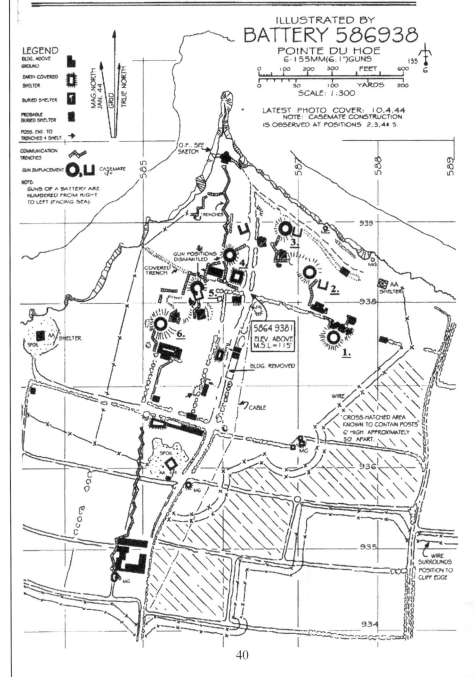

ILLUSTRATED BY
BATTERY 586938
POINTE DU HOE
6-155MM(6.1")GUNS

155 / 6

0 100 200 300 FEET 600
0 50 100 YARDS 200
SCALE: 1:300

LATEST PHOTO COVER: 10.4.44
NOTE: CASEMATE CONSTRUCTION
IS OBSERVED AT POSITIONS 2,3,4+5.

LEGEND
BLDG. ABOVE GROUND
EARTH COVERED SHELTER
BURIED SHELTER
PROBABLE BURIED SHELTER
POSS. ENT. TO TRENCHES + SHELT.
COMMUNICATION TRENCHES
GUN EMPLACEMENT   CASEMATE u/c

NOTE:
GUNS OF A BATTERY ARE
NUMBERED FROM RIGHT
TO LEFT (FACING SEA).

MAG. NORTH JAN. 44 / GRID / TRUE NORTH

O.P.. SEE SKETCH

TRENCHES

GUN POSITIONS DISMANTLED

COVERED TRENCH

AA SHELTER

SPOIL

5864 9381
ELEV. ABOVE
M.S.L.=115'

BLDG. REMOVED

CABLE

WIRE

CROSS-HATCHED AREA
KNOWN TO CONTAIN POSTS
6' HIGH APPROXIMATELY
50' APART.

SPOIL

WIRE SURROUNDS
POSITION TO
CLIFF EDGE

585 587 588 589
939
938
936
935
934

MG
MG
MG
MG

40

lower-level air attacks, the fire of the 20mm guns was supplemented by machine-gun fire from stand-alone *Tobrukstand* positions and other positions built into a number of the casemates. All of these had dual-purpose ground/anti-aircraft mounts.

Progress was slow as the Eastern European 'volunteer labour' (*Hilfswillige*) was limited, resources in the form of steel and concrete were slow in arriving and construction engineers and their cement-mixers too few. There was, however, a limit to the amount of work that the infantry and gunners could undertake before the technical construction of the steel for the reinforced concrete was needed. None the less, monitored by Allied air photography, work progressed and by May 1944 two of the casemates were standing and the footings for a further two casemates was under way.

Admiral Kirk's report on the ground defences nicely describes those at Pointe du Hoc:

All battery positions except temporary field positions had underground shelters and living quarters interconnected with the gun emplacement by well-camouflaged communication trenches, and were protected by machine guns and anti-tank

One of the *Tobrukstands* at Pointe du Hoc today. The crater behind it is from a near miss by a 500lb bomb or a 14in shell.

A German machine-gunner occupying a *Tobrukstand.*

guns, always surrounded by bands of wire and often with bands of mines. In general, the concrete was 6 to 7 feet thick reinforced with ½-inch round rods spaced 9″ on centers horizontally and vertically; the quality of the concrete appeared excellent and the workmanship exceptional; roof slabs were consistently poured onto steel plates which formed the ceilings of the shelters and casemates. In certain cases, for larger caliber guns, roof slabs were as thick as 12 feet.

In late May, although the two casemates were ostensibly complete they, like the battery command post, had not been commissioned; i.e. electrics, communications, ventilation and most steel doors had not all been delivered or fitted. In the case of the command post, the battery's observers had been operating from a trench alongside the new structure until immediately before D-Day, when it and a chunk of cliff were blown down onto the beach.

The attentions of the Allied air forces from 16 April 1944 onwards had also played a part in slowing construction work, with bombers from the 9th US Air Force and RAF Bomber Command making further strikes on 25 April and 22 May. Air Operation Order No. 3-44 outlines the aim of the pre-D-Day bombing programme:

The temporary command post on the cliff next to the new but unfinished bunker.

General priority for the fire support program is given to the neutralization or destruction of Forces. Batteries covering the sea approaches and the beaches are regarded as primary targets for the heavy night and medium bombers ... attacks on batteries will be confined to those in open emplacements or under construction, with a view to harassing rather than destructive effect.

During one of these three raids, it is alleged that one of the guns had been damaged and was possibly the one found off-site on D-Day by the Rangers. Its loss probably convinced the battalion commander to redeploy the remaining gun to the alternative position on the reverse slope some 1,000 yards inland. While most of the 85 gunners left the battery site, the 125 infantrymen remained in *Stützpunkt* 75 ready to man the defences.

The local French Resistance and their historians insist that they had passed word to London in April and in May regarding the location of the guns in the orchards between D514 and La Montagne Farm but despite this, the Allied intelligence staff believed immediately before D-Day that the guns were still in place.

The Allied 1:12,500 and 1:25,000 BIGOT Top Secret Defences Overprint maps issued early in May correctly showed only two guns in position and four casemates U/C (under construction). However, the 'Stop Press' edition of 20 May 1944 shows that the three easterly guns were back and that the westerly gun was still in position. Given that we believe the guns had been moved earlier, how can this be reconciled with photographic evidence? Some 80 per cent of intelligence on the Atlantic Wall was gained from air photography, often taken from a considerable altitude, and mis-interpretations were found to have been common once the army had 'boots on the ground'. In this case the Germans had simply set up telegraph poles and piled other materials to represent the carriages and provide the distinctive signature of a large artillery piece.

The issue of whether the six Pointe du Hoc guns were present or not and when they had been removed or returned is really a secondary issue but is one that still rumbles on today. The fact is that with the air photo interpreters claiming on the Defences Over-print map 'Stop Press' edition of 22 May and older conflicting information about the guns' removal from the Resistance, after considerable debate Generals Bradley and Gerow were simply not

US A-20 Havoc medium bombers attacking Pointe du Hoc in a daylight raid on 15 April 1944.

The clifftop hit by a bomb in the raid of 15 April. See the Defences Overprint for the annotation 'BOMB DAMAGE'.

prepared to take a risk. This was, after all, a powerful battery that had the potential to engage OMAHA and the approaches to both American beaches. They wanted to guarantee that the guns were out of action as V US Corps stormed ashore and the only way to do that as far as the army was concerned, despite the assurances of the navies and air forces that they could do the job, was to have boots on the ground. In addition, changes to the plan at such a late stage were increasingly difficult to make, so the assault on Pointe du Hoc would go ahead as planned.

To add another level to this saga, the evidence of air photography was believed over that being supplied by the local French Resistance. Cropping up frequently in Intelligence documents issued prior to D-Day is the phrase 'Unreliable sources state ...' This sums up the view that the Allies, particularly the British, had of the Resistance and explains why they would trust the evidence of their own high-altitude photography over observations at ground level.

There is a fifth gun shown on the Defences Overprint of which there is no record at Pointe du Hoc. If it was there, as in other

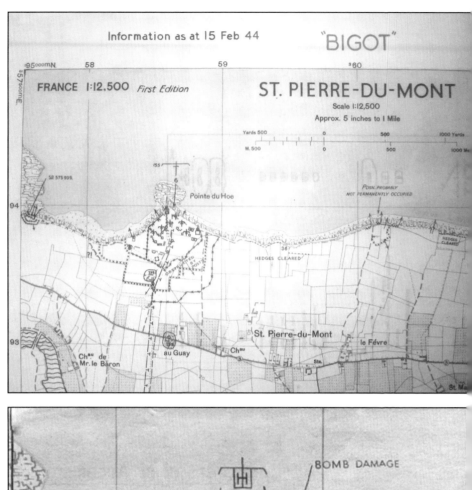

95 000mN   58   59   ³60

FRANCE 1:12,500 *First Edition*   **ST. PIERRE-DU-MONT**

Scale 1:12,500
Approx. 5 inches to 1 Mile

Yards 500   0   500   1000 Yards
M. 500   0   500   1000 M.

SR 575 939.

Pointe du Hoe

POSN. PROBABLY
NOT PERMANENTLY OCCUPIED

HEDGES
CLEARED

94

?1

HEDGES CLEARED

36

93

St. Pierre-du-Mont

le Févre

Ch^au de
Mr. le Baron

au Guay

Ch^au

Sta.

St. Ma

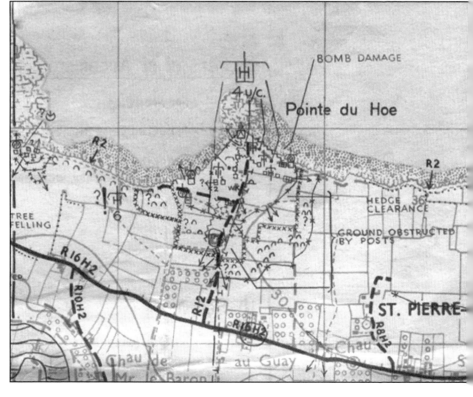

BOMB DAMAGE

4 u/c.

Pointe du Hoe

R2

R2

TREE
FELLING

HEDGE 36
CLEARANCE

GROUND OBSTRUCTED
BY POSTS

R 16 H2

R 10 H2

R 12

R 16 H2

30

ST. PIERRE-

R 8 H2

Ch^au de
Mr. le Baron

au Guay

Ch^au

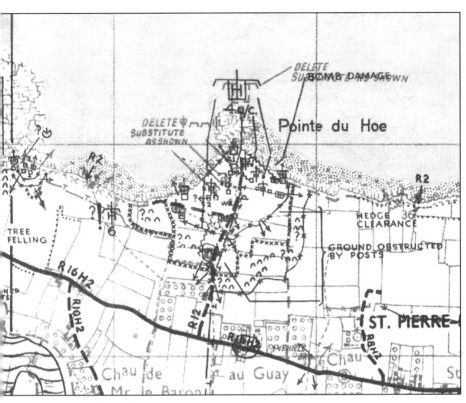

Defences Overprint sequence.

A dummy gun set up in one of the remaining gun-pits.

47

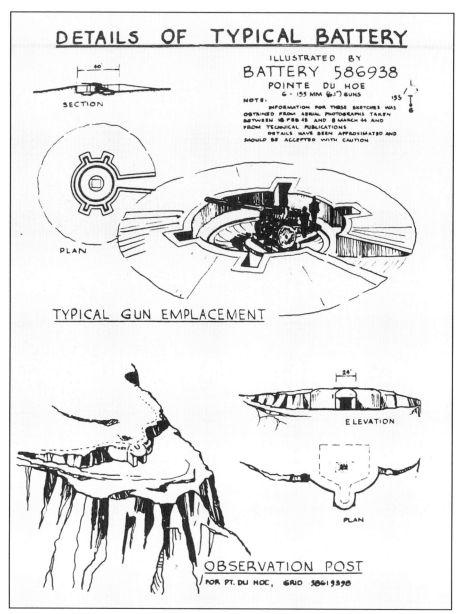

DETAILS OF TYPICAL BATTERY

ILLUSTRATED BY
BATTERY 586938
POINTE DU HOE
6 - 155 MM (6.1") GUNS

NOTE:
INFORMATION FOR THESE SKETCHES WAS OBTAINED FROM AERIAL PHOTOGRAPHS TAKEN BETWEEN 18 FEB 43 AND 8 MARCH 44 AND FROM TECHNICAL PUBLICATIONS
DETAILS HAVE BEEN APPROXIMATED AND SHOULD BE ACCEPTED WITH CAUTION

60'

SECTION

PLAN

TYPICAL GUN EMPLACEMENT

24'

ELEVATION

PLAN

OBSERVATION POST
FOR PT. DU HOC, GRID 58619398

Features of the Pointe du Hoc Battery as shown in the Neptune Monograph.

batteries of the 1260th Army Artillery Battalion such as at nearby Longues-sur-Mer, this is likely to be a French 75mm intended to be used to fire illuminating rounds out to sea at night, presumably linking in with the nearby coastal radar sites.

OMAHA Beach

As this book is focused on the actions of Rudder's Provisional Ranger Group, only the most westerly portion of OMAHA Beach (DOG Sector) and the adjacent Charlie Sector will be covered in this section.

General Gerow's V US Corps planners were confident that with the aid of a heavy bombardment the GIs from the 1st and 29th US Infantry divisions would be able to get up the sloping 80ft to 120ft-high bluffs that rose behind OMAHA Beach for the entire 5 miles, broken only by a number of valleys or draws leading inland from the beach. However, they had a problem at the very western end of the beach and that was a clifftop position that mutually supported the network of *Widerstandsnest* (Wn 71 and 72) that blocked and covered the Vierville-sur-Mer draw, known as DOG 1. This position, it was considered, would need the assistance of Rangers and their expertise in cliff-climbing to out-flank.

General Gerow, the commander of V US Corps.

This small position was known to the Germans as *Widerstands-nest* 73 (Wn 73) and to the Allies as Fortified House after the ruins of a building in a small fold in the cliff. It consisted of either an old French 75mm or a captured Russian 100mm gun (sources and evidence disagree), machine guns, two or three mortars, troop shelters and an artillery/mortar observer's position, all of which could very effectively enfilade the entire western portion of OMAHA Beach. The whole position was connected up with trenches and sur-rounded on the landward side by mines and barbed wire. The cliff face, as at Pointe du Hoc, was believed to be booby-trapped with shells.

Beyond Wn 73 was a small defensive position site at Pointe et Raz de la Percée whose main armament was a pair of 76.2mm artillery pieces sited to fire onto the western end of OMAHA. Next, 1,000 yards further to the west, were the defences around the

49

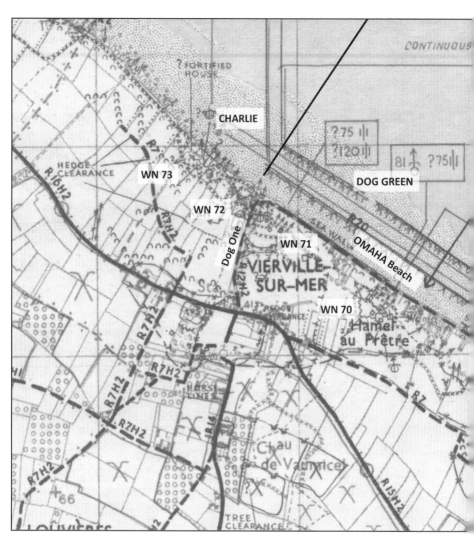

An extract from the Defences Overprint map of the western end of OMAHA Beach.

sizeable radar station at Semaphore, principally three 20mm anti-aircraft guns. The remainder of the 5 miles of unbroken cliffs to Pointe du Hoc was covered by four small infantry section positions with at least a pair of machine guns each.

To the front of the German strongpoints, the belts of wire and the minefields, was the open expanse of the beach and obstacles designed to destroy landing craft in the water. The German estimate was that the Allied assault would be led by infantry who would land at high water in order to reduce the distance across an

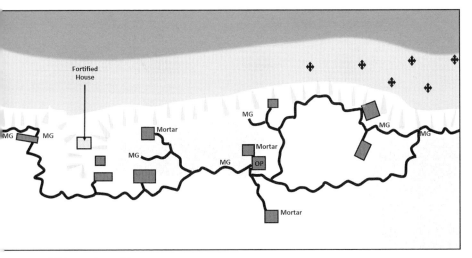

Widerstandsnest 73.

exposed beach. Therefore the obstacles were set out in several rows between 12ft and 17ft above the low-tide mark and were designed to impede a landing at high water.

Most of the material used in constructing beach obstacles was scavenged from border fortifications of the occupied countries. Czech hedgehogs (jagged steel cruciform), curved girders from the Maginot Line and even steel gates from Belgian border crossings would, on a rising tide, be a test of the Allied landing craft crew.

Oberstleutnant Fritz Ziegelmann, chief of staff of the 352nd Division, described the work undertaken by his division on the OMAHA front:

> Assuming that enemy landings would only take place at high tide, obstacles of all kinds were erected on the top part of the beach, so that their upper parts projected from the sea. 'Tschechen' [hedgehog] defences, pile-driven stakes of metal, and concrete as well as wooden trestles were set up here and partly charged with deep water or surface mines and HE shells.
>
> During the storms in April, the mass of these obstacles were torn out and the mines exploded. It was necessary to begin again. Considering that the wood had to be cut in the Forêt de Cerisy, carried at least 30 kilometres in horse-drawn vehicles (lack of fuel), had to be logged by circular saw (limited supply) and rammed by hand (which took a long time), and was particularly difficult on account of the rocky foreground, results were surprisingly good.

51

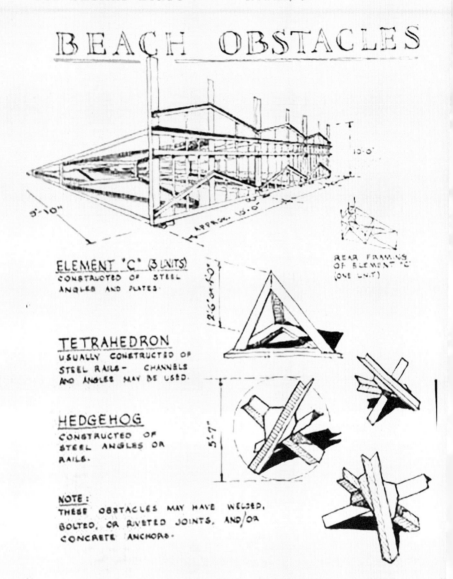

BEACH OBSTACLES

ELEMENT "C" (3 UNITS)
CONSTRUCTED OF STEEL
ANGLES AND PLATES.

REAR FRAMING
OF ELEMENT "C"
(ONE UNIT)

TETRAHEDRON
USUALLY CONSTRUCTED OF
STEEL RAILS - CHANNELS
AND ANGLES MAY BE USED.

HEDGEHOG
CONSTRUCTED OF
STEEL ANGLES OR
RAILS.

NOTE:
THESE OBSTACLES MAY HAVE WELDED,
BOLTED, OR RIVETED JOINTS, AND/OR
CONCRETE ANCHORS.

NEPTUNE MONOGRAPH-CTF 122

TOP SECRET-BIGOT

An illustration of beach obstacles from the Monograph.

In the second half of May, the possibility of a landing at low water was discussed. The construction of obstacles to the seaward of the existing coastal defences was begun but it was impossible to build these obstacles in proper density.

In post-war interviews, despite his positive report on the state of training in the division, *Oberstleutnant* Ziegelmann complained that all this labouring had seriously retarded the training of what was a newly-raised division.

The Final Days

Now well into the period where an invasion could be expected, the Germans continued all along the coast to work on improving their defences. With, however, the increasing tempo of Allied bombing, both by day and night, in the final days of May into the first days of June, work was slow. So as to maintain the Allied deception plan (Operation FORTITUDE NORTH) for as long as possible, only one-third of the tonnage of bombs dropped during this period was delivered to targets in Normandy. Despite this, Pointe du Hoc, clearly a priority target, received no fewer than three major air-raids during this period culminating on 4 June, with the results being photographed by Mustang aircraft of 109 (Reconnaissance) Squadron USAAF, known as 'The Lookers', flying from Middle Wallop.

Despite the increasing Allied air activity in early May, with thirty-two *Widerstandsnest* and *Stützpunkt* between the Rivers Vire and Dives complete or nearly so, Rommel wrote to his wife: 'I am more confident than ever before. If the British give us just two more weeks, I won't have any more doubt about it.' Finally, just two weeks before D-Day Rommel issued a morale-raising Order of the

Rommel during one of his inspections.

An oblique air photograph taken in late 1943, early in the planning process.

Day that also reflected his own growing confidence in the outcome of an Allied attack on the Atlantic Wall:

I have expressed my deep appreciation of the well-planned and well-executed work performed in so few months.

The main defence zone on the coast is strongly fortified and well manned; there are large tactical and operational reserves in the area. Thousands of pieces of artillery, anti-tank guns, rocket projectiles and flame-throwers await the enemy; millions of mines under water and on land lie in wait for him.

In spite of the enemy's great air superiority, we can face coming events with the greatest confidence.

ROMMEL
Field Marshal
22 May 44

Chapter Three

The D-Day Ranger Plan

Following the Casablanca Conference in late January 1943, a compromise was made between the British desire to pursue the war in the Mediterranean and the US determination to defeat Germany as quickly as possible and then get on with the war against Japan in its 'Pacific back yard'. In this negotiation, the British were firmly committed to the invasion of North-West Europe in 1944 in exchange for knocking Italy out of the war in 1943. Taking on Italy would not only diminish the prestige of the Axis but also have the beneficial effect of forcing Germany to replace hundreds of thousands of Italian troops in garrisons across the Balkans and in Italy itself. This would in turn help relieve pressure on the Red Army on the Eastern Front and satisfy Stalin that he was not the only Ally fighting.

The British Lieutenant General Sir Frederick Morgan was appointed as Chief of Staff Supreme Allied Commander (Designate) or COSSAC in March 1943, with Brigadier General Ray

Lieutenant General Sir Frederick Morgan, COSSAC (Designate).

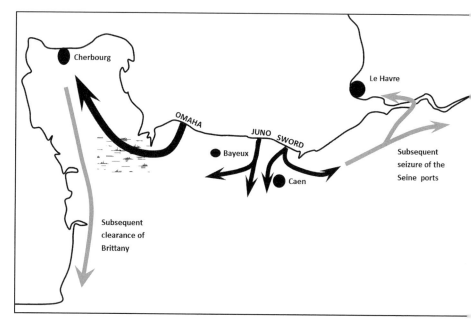

The original COSSAC plan.

Barker being his US military deputy. Initially, the planning HQ was established at Norfolk House in St James's Square but by October 1943, the headquarters had grown to 320 British and American officers of all services and branches plus 600 other ranks.

The COSSAC plan was for a landing on a relatively narrow front, the original three beaches for the Americans, Canadians and British being OMAHA, JUNO and SWORD. General Montgomery, who was nominated as commander of the 21st Army Group having handed over the Eighth Army, was shown the plan on New Year's Eve 1943 by Churchill in North Africa. Taking the documents to bed, partly to avoid a late night with the prime minister, Montgomery did not like the plan and in a closely-argued memo submitted by him the following morning he listed the main difficulties, which were that it was on a narrow front that would allow the Germans to concentrate against the Allied beachhead and that it was far too far for the Americans from OMAHA Beach to the all-important port of Cherbourg, with, in addition, the rivers and marshes around Carentan being a significant obstacle to overcome en route to the vital port.

Once back in London in early January at his HQ at St Paul's School, Montgomery set to work addressing these issues, including placing the US army further west and expanding the First US

Army's beachhead to encompass the two beaches of OMAHA and UTAH. The latter was north of the Carentan Marshes and at the base of the Cotentin Peninsula, with a much-reduced distance to Cherbourg.

The problem with this plan, which was accepted by General Eisenhower, was that it would delay D-Day while more troops were trained and equipped for the upscaled invasion. Not only that, there was a dangerous German coastal battery shown on the tactical overprint maps that were beginning to be produced at Pointe du Hoe [*sic*].

General Sir Bernard Montgomery.

(In copying the French maps, the engravers of the printing plate miscopied the name, spelling it with an 'e' instead of Pointe du Hoc.) Also shown on these maps were three further battery positions around the village of Maisy near Grandcamp, which at that time were thought to also mount 155mm guns. Together they represented a significant challenge to the planners.

With the upscaling of Operation OVERLORD, the difficulties of establishing a beachhead inland from UTAH Beach for the VII US

The 21st Army Group's revised plan.

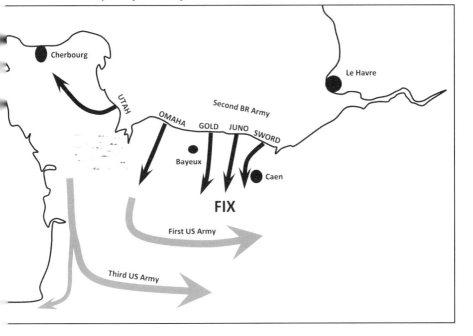

Senior Allied commanders.

Corps, thanks to German inundations, were considerable. In addition, a link-up between V and VII corps astride extensive marshes at the mouths of the rivers Vire and Taute was going to require the two US airborne divisions.

While General Montgomery's changes to the COSSAC plan had been agreed by General Eisenhower and the senior Allied commanders who would have to execute them, Lieutenant Colonel Rudder, who had been given 'BIGOT' top-secret clearance to know the extraordinarily closely-guarded secret of the 'where' and the 'when' of D-Day was summoned to London. Only a few tactical commanders with highly specific tasks requiring special training and preparations were briefed as early in the process as Rudder. In January 1944, he and the then Major Max Schneider reported to Headquarters First US Army to personally receive his orders from General Omar Bradley, who later recalled his feelings about briefing Rudder on his Operation OVERLORD mission:

> No soldier in my command has ever been wished a more dif-
> ficult task than that which befell the 34-year-old commander

of this Provisional Ranger Force. Lieutenant Colonel James E. Rudder, a rancher from Brady, Texas, was to take a force of 200 men, land on a shingled shelf under the face of a 100-foot cliff, scale the cliff, and there destroy an enemy battery of coastal guns.

Rudder later told General Bradley: 'The first time you mentioned it, I thought you were trying to scare me.' Major Schneider was also at the meeting and with the experience of three landings in the Mediterranean behind him, whistled through his teeth at the thought of the challenges that they were going to face.

The two US Ranger battalions were to be formed into the Provisional Ranger Group under command of Lieutenant Colonel Rudder. Their mission was to be completed by 0700 hours, thirty minutes after the US landing on OMAHA and UTAH beaches. Even though putting the guns out of action before the landing would have been desirable and the US airborne divisions would have already been on the ground, General Gerow, the commander of V US Corps, felt that an early attack on Pointe du Hoc and its proximity to OMAHA Beach would compromise any tactical surprise he might achieve. In addition, as the plan developed there were obvious and significant difficulties inherent in a night-time assault.

General Omar Bradley, the commander of the First US Army.

General Gerow, the commander of V US Corps.

The Ranger Plan

For operational control, the Provisional Ranger Group was placed under command of the 116th US Infantry Regiment (detached from the 29th US ID), who were themselves under command of the 1st US Infantry Division, until their parent formation's HQ was ashore, which was scheduled for later on D-Day.

The initial iteration of the Rangers' orders is shown on the map on p. 62. Note the plentiful use of the words 'reconnoiter' and 'observe'. By the time the plan was fully developed, there had clearly been a significant migration from intelligence-gathering to offensive action and the insertion of additional offensive tasks. This was by no means an unusual phenomenon, as more officers were 'BIGOTed' and therefore able to look at the operation and its problems in greater detail. This first iteration also reveals General Gerow's lack of early understanding of the Rangers and their capability.

Eventually, Rudder's D-Day task was in many ways similar to that of the British Commandos; i.e. the taking of coastal batteries and clearing opposition to the flanks of the beaches and assisting the link-up between the leading formations. This was designed to allow the infantry divisions to focus on reaching beachhead objectives as far as 8 miles inland without worrying too much about enemy activity on the coastal strip. In the case of V US Corps at OMAHA, things did not of course turn out like that but that was the commander's ultimate intent for the Rangers in his plan.

Lieutenant Colonel Rudder was told that he would be attacking following an overnight raid on Pointe du Hoc by RAF Bomber Command, a bombardment by USS *Texas* (ten 14in guns) and HMS *Talybont*, a Hunt-class destroyer (four 4.4in guns), and finally a bombing raid by eighteen medium bombers of the Ninth US Air Force as late as twenty minutes before the Rangers were to land. Following the assault US and Royal Navy destroyers with 4in to 5in guns would also be on call to bombard Pointe du Hoc if necessary. This 'drenching fire' was designed to shock and stun the defenders so as to downgrade the defensive capability at the time of landing.

A study of the problem of Pointe du Hoc and planning for the operation had been under way before Rudder had been briefed. It was largely developed by a Combined Operations staff officer, Colonel Richardson. His plan reflecting the intelligence nature of

USS *Texas*.

the early plan was for two landings, one at Grandcamp to the west and on OMAHA Beach 4 miles to the east, combined with a para-chute drop by just thirty-five men on Pointe du Hoc itself. Later it was intended that they would neutralize the battery while the main attacking forces broke in from the landward flanks. A clifftop para-chute drop would, however, have been risky and not been relished by the airborne commanders. General Gerow was also against the use of paratroopers, probably thinking about the dispersed drop in Sicily, and he thought it unlikely that they could be dropped with sufficient accuracy for such an important task.

With the airborne divisions fully committed and General Gerow ruling them out as the key part of the plan, the assault forces faced the prospect of breaking into the battery through thick barbed-wire obstacles, a minefield, in daylight and under fire from machine guns mounted in *Tobrukstands* and atop various bunkers. In contrast with the less heavily-defended Merville Battery, which was to be attacked by the British 6th Airborne Division, the Rangers were being tasked to achieve the same result without the cover of dark-ness or tactical surprise. It is not surprising that the plan was promptly rejected.

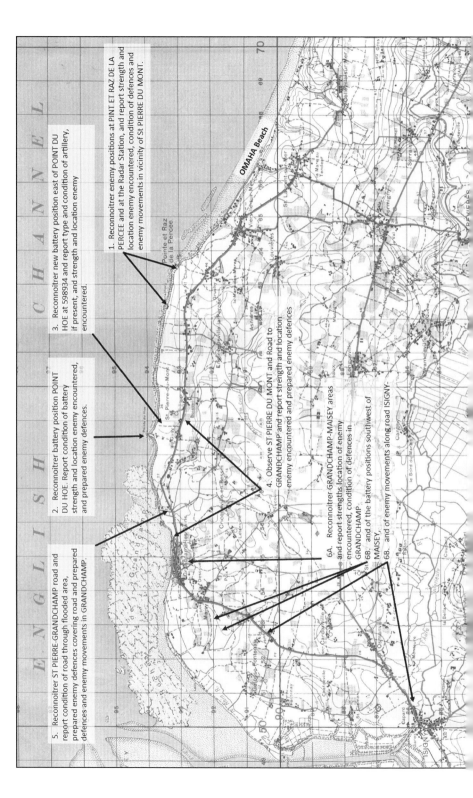

1. Reconnoitre enemy positions at PINT ET RAZ DE LA PERCEE and at the Radar Station, and report strength and location enemy encountered, condition of defences and enemy movements in vicinity of St PIERRE DU MONT.

3. Reconnoitre new battery position east of POINT DU HOE at 598934 and report type and condition of artillery, if present, and strength and location enemy encountered.

2. Reconnoitre battery position POINT DU HOE. Report condition of battery strength and location enemy encountered, and prepared enemy defences.

4. Observe ST PIERRE DU MONT and road to GRANDCHAMP and report strength and location enemy encountered and prepared enemy defences

5. Reconnoitre ST PIERRE-GRANDCHAMP road and report condition of road through flooded area, prepared enemy defences covering road and prepared enemy movements in GRANDCHAMP.

6A. Reconnoitre GRANDCHAMP-MAISEY areas and report strengths location of enemy encountered, condition of defences in GRANDCHAMP.
6B. and of the battery positions southwest of MAISEY,
6B. and of enemy movements along road ISIGNY-

OMAHA Beach

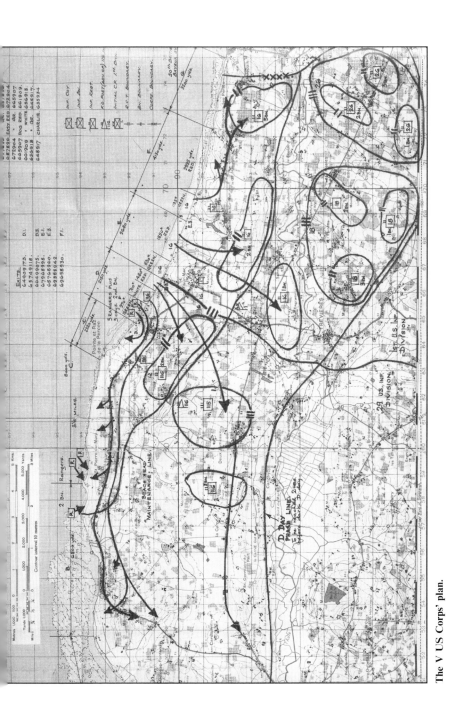

The V US Corps' plan.

Lieutenant Colonel Rudder and Max Schneider, having been briefed on their task, took over planning with the assistance of their experienced British Commando advisor and liaison officer Lieutenant Colonel Tom Trevor, who was attached to the Rangers principally to facilitate training. The plan that Rudder developed was an initial assault up the cliff, astride the point, by three companies of the 2nd Battalion (Ranger Force A). They would be accompanied by a Naval Shore Fire Control Party (NSFCP) that was to control the fire of the destroyers including USS *Satterlee* and HMS *Talybont* when required inland. A forward observation party attached from the 58th Armoured Field Artillery Battalion would land with Company E. Their 105mm guns were scheduled to be ashore around 0800 hours on DOG Beach and would be able to support the Rangers once they were within range of the Pointe, i.e. just over 5,000 yards.

When the plan based on an assault directly up the cliffs was proposed in Admiral Hall's headquarters, an Intelligence staff officer famously uttered: 'It can't be done! Three old women with brooms could keep the Rangers from climbing that cliff.' With an equally impossible alternative already rejected and with cliff-climbing

An air recce photo of the western face of the Pointe annotated by an interpreter.

being already high on the training agenda of the two Ranger battalions, Lieutenant Colonel Trevor and Headquarters Commando Group were consulted. They confirmed that with the Rangers already free-climbing the Cornish cliffs in the dark it was very much possible!

Lieutenant Colonel Rudder's plan was given further impetus when it was discovered that the Germans were inundating the low ground to the west between Grandcamp and the battery and that the inundation could well extend into the valley a mile south of the battery. By D-Day this was substantially the case.

The original plan was that the rest of the Provisional Ranger Force would head for OMAHA and infiltrate west to relieve the companies at Pointe du Hoc. However, during exercises on the South Devon coast this proved to be unwieldy and was revised.

The revised plan was that once the battery was secure, the 2nd Rangers' tactical HQ up with the Assault Company would send the code-word 'CROWBAR' or 'PRAISE THE LORD' to call in Ranger Force C to land below the eastern face of the Pointe. First ashore would be two companies of the 2nd Rangers, Companies A and B, who were the leading element of Ranger Force C. They would be followed thirty minutes later by Max Schneider's 5th Rangers (the remainder of Ranger Force C), with a second NSFCP and a Forward Air Control Party. Rudder argued that this would make a powerful force available to take on the enemy 4 miles to the west of OMAHA Beach and suck in German reserves.

The US Center for Military History outlines the intent in the case of failure to take Pointe du Hoc:

An alternate plan was ready if the support force of Rangers had not received word, by H+30, of success in the attack on the cliffs at Pointe du Hoe [*sic*]. In this event, the larger Ranger force would land on the western end of OMAHA Beach (Vierville sector) behind the 116th Infantry and proceed overland towards the Pointe, avoiding all unnecessary action en route to its objective.

In the event of diversion provision was made for the battalions to fit into the 116th Infantry's OMAHA Beach landing table. Once ashore, however, they were to infiltrate to a rendezvous beyond Vierville from where they would march to Pointe du Hoc by minor roads.

LANDING DIAGRAM, OMAHA BEACH

(SECTOR OF 116th RCT)

	EASY GREEN	DOG RED	DOG WHITE	DOG GREEN
H-5			Co C (SD) 743 Tk Bn	Co B (DD) 743 Tk Bn
HHOUR	Co A 743 Tk Bn	Co A 743 Tk Bn		
H+01	Co E 116 Inf	Co F 116 Inf	Co G 116 Inf	Co A 116 Inf
H+03	146 Engr CT	146 Engr GT / Demolitions Control Boat	146 Engr CT	146 Engr CT / Co C 2d Ranger Bn
H+30	AAAW Btry / CoH HQCoE CoH 116 Inf / AAAW Bry	HQ 2d Bn / CoH CoF CoH / HQ / 2d Bn / 16 Inf / AAAW Btry	AAAW Btry / CoH HQCoG CoH / 116 Inf / AAAW Btry	Co B HQCoA Co B / HQ / 116 Inf / AAAW Btry
H+40	112 Engr Bn	112 Engr / Co D 81 Cml Wpns Bn / 149 Engr Beach Bn	149 Engr Beach Bn 121 Engr Bn	HQ / 1st Bn 16 / 149 Beach Bn 121 Engr / Co D 116 Inf
H+50	Co L 116 Inf	Co I 116 Inf	Co K 116 Inf	121 Engr Bn / Co C 116 Inf
H+57		HQ Co 3d Bn / Co M 116 Inf		Co B 81 Cml Wpns Bn
H+60		112 Engr Bn	HQ a 116 Co 116 Inf	121 Engr Bn / Co A a B 2d Ranger Bn
H+65				5th Ranger Bn
H+70	149 Engr Beach Bn	112 Engr Bn	Alt HQ a HQ Co 116 Inf	121 Engr Bn / 5th Ranger Bn
H+90			58 FA Bn Armd	
H+100			6th Engr Sp Brig	
H+110	111 FA Bn (3 Btry's in DUKWS)	AT Plat 2d Bn AT Plat 3d Bn / 29 Sig Bn		AT Plat 1st Bn Cn Co 116 Inf
H+120	467 AAAW Bn Cn Co 116 Inf 467 AAAW Bn	AT Co 116 Inf / 467 AAAW Bn 149 Engr Beach Bn	467 AAAW Bn	467 AAAW Bn
H+150		DD Tanks	HQ Co 116 Inf / 104 Med Bn	
H+180 to H+215		461 Amphibious Track Co	Navy Salvage	
H+225	461 Amph Trk Co			

LCI | LCM | LCA | DD Tank
LCT | LCVP | DUKW

Note: Plan as of 11 May

The 116th Infantry's landing diagram.

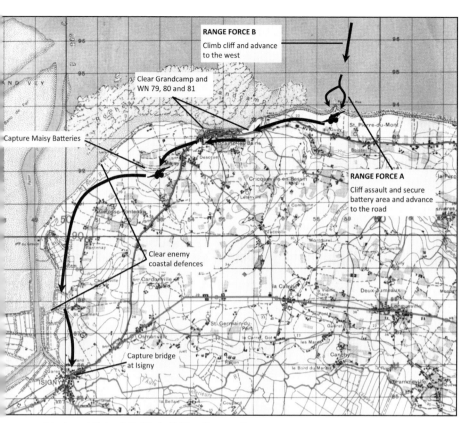

Lieutenant Colonel Rudder's D-Day Ranger plan.

Meanwhile, Captain Goranson's Company C, 2nd Rangers (Ranger Force B) had the separate mission on the cliffs at the western end of OMAHA Beach (Wn 73).

Having taken and secured the battery by 0700 hours, the presence of the Rangers just a few hundred yards from the D514 coastal road would naturally inhibit German reinforcements heading from the area between Isigny and Grandcamp-Maisy towards OMAHA Beach. Although not found explicitly in Rudder's orders from the 1st Division, this could be an implied task or possibly one requested by the 116th US Infantry as it would force the Germans to take a detour around their own inundation to the west of Grandcamp via Cricqueville-en-Bessin.

Lieutenant Colonel Rudder, as provisional group commander, was ordered not to take part in the assault on the Pointe but was to exercise overall control of the operation from General Gerow's by now veteran headquarters ship USS *Ancon*. Consequently, the officer commanding Company A, Captain Lytle, took over command of Ranger Force A.

The leading elements of the 116th were scheduled to reach the Rangers at Pointe du Hoc from OMAHA Beach by 1200 hours, at which point with the 5th Rangers leading they would advance with the 1st Battalion, 116th Infantry west on Wn 76, 77 and clear Grandcamp.

The Rangers' British Commando Bergan-style rucksacks were to come ashore in the battalion's transport during the night of D-Day and were expected to join up with the rest of the Ranger force somewhere near Grandcamp on D+1.

The sheer difficulty of the task of getting up the cliffs meant that the casualties, already expected to be high among the assault troops, were elevated to no less than 70 per cent for the Provisional Ranger Group. Consequently, with the detail of the training being left to Lieutenant Colonel Trevor and his executive officer (second-in-command), the combat-experienced Major Schneider, Lieutenant Colonel Rudder focused on recruiting and training sufficient battle casualty replacements to keep the 2nd and 5th battalions viable post-D-Day.

Equipment

With the mission and plan made, Rudder set about devising the method of attack. The most significant challenge, exactly as predicted by Admiral Hall's staff officer, was to get up the cliff and into the battery without being 'swept off'. The Rangers would have not only to face the enemy but the cliff itself. It was not the solid granite of the Cornish cliffs or the firm chalk of Freshwater Bay but a crumbling cliff of alternate bands of honey-coloured limestone and loose mudstone! Locating a geologically-similar cliff at West Bay near Bridport on the Dorset coast, with the help of Lieutenant Colonel Trevor, it was obvious that conventional methods of climbing would not work on such a cliff. Alternatives had to be found.

It was obvious that the unstable 100ft cliff was too tall for the 4ft-long sectionalized aluminium commando ladders to be practical. These lightweight tubular ladders, which were designed to be fitted together, simply became unstable the more they were extended. The Rangers found that by adapting and securely pre-assembling them into 16ft lengths the wobble was reduced, but even so it was a far too tenuous method to be relied upon.

The cliffs just to the east of Pointe du Hoc were of exactly the same crumbly nature as the Pointe.

With necessity being the mother of invention, all kinds of methods of getting up the cliff were considered including a naval barrage balloon but the obvious frailty of this idea along with others was quickly ruled out as impractical. Other solutions were required. Fortunately, the fertile minds of scientists and engineers working for the Headquarters Combined Operations Miscellaneous Weapons Development Department had some time earlier started working on a project to fire ropes to the top of a cliff with rocket-powered grapples. However, with no conceivable use for them in the foreseeable future the project had been shelved.

At the request of Commando Headquarters, work on two versions was restarted as a matter of considerable priority. They were soon under development: a larger, heavier rocket that was to be mounted on the ten British-crewed Landing Craft Assault (LCAs) to be used by Ranger Force A in its run-in to the cliffs; six per craft were to be mounted in pairs on the bow, amidships and at the stern. Each LCA had two of the lighter versions that could be carried ashore by the Rangers and fired from the narrow beach at the foot of the cliff.

It would be a strenuous way up the cliff, suitable for only lightly-armed and equipped Rangers. A method to get Ranger Force A's packs, radios, heavy weapons and ammunition up and quickly available for action was needed and of course Ranger Force C needed to be at the top of the cliff as quickly as possible to help defend against the expected counter-attacks and to prepare for their subsequent tasks. The solution, another Combined Operations idea, was a steady 100ft ladder up which several laden men could climb at the same time. The only such ladders in the United

The lighter of the two types of rocket-powered grapples.

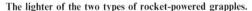

Kingdom were the extendable London Fire Brigade escape ladders. Four of these ladders, one for each assault company and a reserve, were requisitioned and mounted on the 3-ton amphibious truck the DUKW (commonly known as the Duck) and code-named SWAN.

The aim was to drive the DUKW on to the beach and using power from the engine start to extend the ladder, with a Ranger at the top manning twin Vickers-K guns. Landing just behind the LCAs, the SWANs could quickly be deployed and if necessary provide suppressive fire onto the clifftop and into the battery when fully extended while Rangers climbed up below the machine-gunner. The problem was that the DUKWs would not be available until just before the invasion was due to be launched.

A SWAN photographed during training with a Ranger manning the twin Vickers guns.

The lengths of aluminium Commando ladders would be taken strapped to the top sides of the Landing Craft as 'belt and braces', possibly because it was clear from the photographs taken after the April bombing raid that at least one section of the cliff had been brought down, forming a ramp up from the beach that could present an opportunity to use ladders.

Of the preparation of equipment, the commander of the Western Task Force (TF-122) stated in his report on the operation as a whole (but equally applicable to Pointe du Hoc):

> The planning continued for a period which was long enough to permit material and operational experiments to be carried out to test the practicability of the planners' ideas. These experiments covered material ones conducted in the various weapons and landing craft under a wide set of circumstances as well as exercises carried out by troop units and specialized parties organized for the accomplishment of new types of missions.

Training

With his method of getting up the cliff established, Lieutenant Colonel Rudder set about training the Rangers, especially those in Ranger Force A, to climb the plain single ropes, toggle ropes (single ropes with wooden toggles woven into them for hands and feet), and rope ladders on the sheer Dorset cliffs at West Bay and Burton Bradstock. The Rangers in light order, as technique and upper body strength improved, were soon able to scale the cliffs in less than a minute.

The SWANs, crewed by eight soldiers from the 234th Engineer Battalion and five Rangers, found that their unlikely vehicles were able to drive onto the sand and fine shingle beach below the West Bay cliffs. Once ashore, the crew would secure the vehicle with four jacks for stability and start to extend the ladder, ideally at an angle of 60 to 70 degrees in order to make it easier for the Rangers to climb. The Rangers of Force A with heavier weapons and loads were able to be up the cliff in a matter of minutes.

In between climbs the Rangers, now based in a tented camp just outside Dorchester, trained in amphibious assault techniques, weapons training, drills for attacking pill-boxes, demolitions and of course maintaining fitness. The scale of training was growing and the Rangers found themselves taking part in Exercise FABIUS I, just one part of the complex rehearsals for D-Day. During this

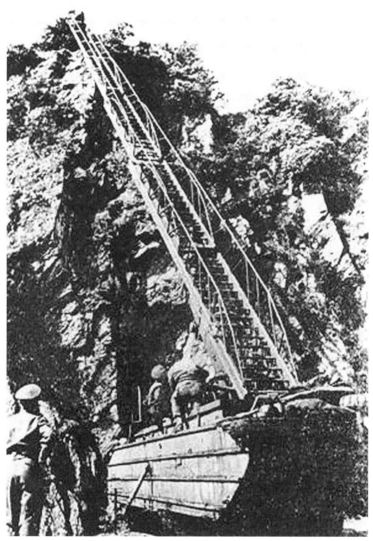

A SWAN photographed during cliff assault training.

exercise, the Rangers made the acquaintance of the mother ships that would take them across the Channel. Officially they were Landing Ships Infantry (LSIs) but in reality they were a variety of civilian steamers and ferries converted to convey Commandos and Rangers to their trans-shipping point. They had already worked

Rangers photographed during cliff assault training.

with Darby's Rangers in the Mediterranean. Boarding LCAs in Weymouth Harbour, the Rangers were ferried out to LCIs (Landing Craft Infantry) and embarked on their ships in the nearby bay.

Assault Group O4

Unit	Port	Allocation to ships	Remarks
2nd US Rangers	Weymouth	HMS *Prince Charles* (Coys A, B & C & part of HQ 2nd Rangers), SS *Amsterdam* (Coys D & E (-)) SS *Ben-my-Chree* (Coys F, E (-) & part of Force A HQ) LCT No. 46 (2 × SWANs) LCT (2 × SWANs)	Pointe du Hoc/ OMAHA Beach
5th US Rangers	Weymouth	HMS *Prince Baudouin* HMS *Prince Leopold*	Pointe du Hoc/ OMAHA Beach

SS *Ben-my-Chree* before being taken up from trade.

FABIUS was the code-name for the five concurrent assault and one logistic exercises conducted as final rehearsals for D-Day. As far as the combat troops were concerned, each beach had its own exercise. They were designed to simulate the full process of embarking; in the case of FABIUS I, V US Corps aboard the ships of Naval Force O bound for OMAHA Beach. This dress rehearsal was at its early stages, believed by some Rangers to be the real thing!

While the 1st US Infantry Division and elements of the 29th Division landed on Slapton Sands* after spending several days on board ship, the Ranger objective for exercise was atop the Combe Point cliffs just west of Dartmouth in South Devon. These cliffs were not nearly as difficult as those that the Rangers were to tackle at Pointe du Hoc but that was not the point of the exercise, which focused on testing as many of the elements of getting V US Corps to the Normandy coast, ashore onto the beach and staying ashore rather than tactics that were better suited to lower-level exercises.

None the less, an important part of the exercise rehearsed the sequence of landing with Ranger Force A (2nd Rangers' Companies D, E and F) duly sending the signal for success, at which they were followed to the cliff by the leading element of Ranger Force C (2nd Rangers' Companies A and B) who were followed

---

* Only weeks earlier a Force U convoy had been torpedoed by German E-boats sinking or damaging several ships during Exercise Tiger (one of the large-scale rehearsals for the D-Day landings).

Exercise FABIUS I.

thirty minutes later by the 5th Rangers. For Rudder and his men FABIUS I culminated in a 12-mile speed march to simulate the subsequent advance west along the Normandy coast from Pointe du Hoc towards Grandcamp-Maisy.

One of the lessons of the exercise was the need to be able to easily and quickly identify to which battalion a Ranger belonged. Lieutenant Raaen of the 5th Battalion described the solution:

> To prevent such mix-ups, each Ranger had a horizontal, 4-inch orange diamond painted on the rear of his helmet with a black '5' for the 5th Battalion and a '2' for the 2nd. These diamonds helped immensely in keeping integrity under stressful conditions. Non-coms also wore a horizontal one by 3-inch white stripe on the back of their helmets, while officers wore a similar vertical white stripe.

As D-Day approached, the Rangers made a series of moves into the Force O Staging Area, first to Swanage where they could

Ranger officers' D-Day helmet.

continue to train on the Purbeck cliffs with all the scaling means at their disposal. In the middle of the month, however, with training complete the Provisional Ranger Group moved west to camp D-5 (RAF Warmwell) near Dorchester, where increasingly severe restrictions on movement in and out of the camp applied. While in the staging area the Rangers were subject to a thirty-minute air-raid. Such raids were by now a rarity and it was, in most cases, the Rangers' first sight and experience of the enemy but fortunately only a few were lightly wounded.

While in the staging area Lieutenant Colonel Rudder went on a series of trips to finalize details with Major General Huebner, the commanding general of the 1st US Infantry Division, who issued an order that he wanted Rudder and his Provisional Ranger Group Headquarters with him aboard USS *Ancon*, the Naval Force O headquarters ship. However, late in the day he consented to Rudder commanding from HMS *Prince Charles* until his group was ashore.

The final command arrangements and tasks were:

Provisional Ranger Force: Lieutenant Colonel Rudder –
Overall Command.
Ranger Force A: Major Lytle – Initial Assault on Pointe
du Hoc.
Ranger Force B: Captain Goranson – OMAHA Wn 73.
Ranger Force C: Lieutenant Colonel Schneider – Follow on
Pointe du Hoc or OMAHA.

In the camps of the staging area, the process of briefing over
models, sketches and air photographs and the issuing of orders to
company commanders along with the specialist officers began, but
security was tight and 'the need to know principle' strictly enforced.
Meanwhile, to the group as a whole French francs were issued
along with a booklet on France and how to behave with the local
people. So it was to be France but where in France would only be
revealed once the maps with fake names had been withdrawn and
real ones issued when the Rangers were on board their landing
ships.

Chapter Four

Embarkation and Passage

The process of embarking Force O at Weymouth, Portland and Poole Harbour began during the last week of May 1944 and on 1 June it was the Rangers' turn. In common with the Commandos it was intended to keep these troops in the cramped mess decks for as short a time as possible. They were trucked the few miles from their final comfortable camp in the staging area to a drop-off point at the eastern end of Weymouth. From here, fully equipped, they marched along the sea front to the harbour where they fell into the by now familiar process of being ferried out to their ships of Assault Force O-4 waiting for them in Weymouth Bay.

Once aboard the secure confines of the ship, company officers were able to pass on to the ordinary Rangers their briefing, with the help of the latest air photographs and maps issued with the real names. D-Day was set for 5 June 1944 and the Rangers' H-hour was, in common with the rest of the US forces, set at 0630 hours. Further east, the Second British Army's H-hour was an hour later because of a tidal difference.

Rangers making their way down Weymouth promenade to the port.

The 5th Rangers embark in LCAs to be ferried out to their waiting LSIs.

With briefing over, the Rangers in the confined space checked and rechecked their equipment and wrote their traditional final letters home during 3 June. No more training exercises; the next time they weighed anchor they would not be heading west across Lyme Bay to the Devon coast but south to Normandy.

The Wait to Go

Further east from Weymouth at Southwick House, the head-quarters of Admiral Ramsay, the commander of Operation NEPTUNE (the naval part of OVERLORD), General Eisenhower and his senior commanders met at 2100 hours on the evening of 3 June. Here they digested the bad news from their chief meteor-ologist, Group Captain John Stagg, that a weather front would produce strong winds and thick cloud that would hamper if not preclude amphibious landing and prevent effective air and airborne operations during 5 June. Consequently, it was agreed that D-Day would be postponed by twenty-four hours.

On the afternoon of 4 June, the four Landing Ships Infantry (LSIs) of Assault Force O-4 out in Weymouth Bay were being whipped up by the near gale-force winds and the ships were tugging

Southwick House.

uncomfortably on their anchor chains. Consequently, they were moved into the adjacent and already crowded Portland Harbour. Out on deck, the Rangers saw huge breakers hurling themselves against Chesil Bank and even in the sheltered waters of the harbour it was uncomfortable.

Down in the landing ships' crowded mess decks with little room to exercise, Ranger Force A also had an unexpected problem when a significant number went down with a dose of food poisoning believed to be caused by a batch of badly-canned hot dogs. One Ranger recalled:

> It was bad enough having to contend with one's nerves before battle, now the food which they had been served was rancid. The whole battalion was laid low, and many began to doubt if they could go ahead with their mission. Some even suspected their food had been tampered with.

Fortunately these fit, robust young soldiers recovered quickly with little detrimental effect.

During their time on board the ships, news of promotions came in including that of Major Schneider to lieutenant colonel and Captain Lytle to major, reflecting the level of responsibility of the latter officer in commanding Ranger Force A.

Aboard Ranger Force A's headquarters ship, SS *Ben-my-Chree*, an Isle of Man steamer which unlike US ships was not 'dry' and with little else to do other than wait, a celebratory drink in the wardroom bar was in order early in the evening of 4 June. Major Lytle started with a quart of gin and followed this with whisky, the combination of which, together with pre-battle tension, did not make for easy bed-fellows. This mix got the better of the newly-promoted Major Lytle. He became loud, agitated and volubly critical of the Pointe du Hoc mission and plan. Lytle also told his increasingly embarrassed audience that the French Resistance had passed information that the guns had been moved from the Pointe after one of the bombing raids some time earlier and culminated with the remark: 'It's suicide, for Christ's sake.' The whisky had given voice to Major Lytle's concerns; ones shared by many men with the prospect of action for the first time and facing a particularly dangerous task. When restrained by the Rangers' medical officer, Lytle punched him in the face. Having eventually been confined, he was taken below. Rudder aboard HMS *Prince Charles* was informed and sent three captains over to *Ben-my-Chree* to report on the situation.

Major Lytle's behaviour and damaging criticisms, born of uncertain intelligence and a formidable task, meant that he could no longer lead Force A. Consequently, Rudder relieved him of his command and sent him ashore.* Lieutenant Colonel Rudder, however, had a problem. With a difficult command and leadership situation to resolve, he naturally wanted to lead the attack himself but having been specifically ordered by General Huebner to remain in contact aboard HMS *Prince Charles* and only land after Force C, he had little choice but to remain with the Provisional Ranger Group HQ where the question of what to do continued to prey on his mind. Later that evening Rudder went around the force telling his commanders that he would lead the attack, joining the rest of Ranger Force A from HMS *Prince Charles* once the LCAs were launched. In his place Major Sullivan, the executive officer of the

* Major Lytle later became a battalion commander with the 90th US Infantry Division and earned the Distinguished Service Cross in the crossing of the River Mosel.

Amphibious operations headquarters ship USS _Ancon_.

5th Rangers (SS _Prince Baudouin_), would provide the Provisional Ranger Group's rear link to General Huebner aboard the command ship USS _Ancon_.

Even though the intelligence about the guns was not conclusive, General Gerow and Admiral Hall wanted the insurance of boots on the ground, with this extract from Admiral Kirk's TF-122 report demonstrating the extent of reliance on air photography:

> The following types of information of interest to amphibious planning were obtained almost wholly from a study of aerial photographs:
> (1) Location of German Naval Units.
> (2) Numbers and Location of German Aircraft.
> (3) Beach gradients and profiles above LLW [low water].
> (4) Details of roads, exits and terrain features.
> (5) Locations and details of emplacements of coast defence batteries. (Calibers and ranges were determined primarily from ground reports, though physical limitations of traverse were found mainly from aerial photographs.)

The last air photograph issued to the Rangers just before sailing, showing the bombing up to 4 June 1944.

(6) Locations and types of beach obstacles (dimensions of individual obstacles were from ground reports).

(7) Numbers, sizes and locations of beach strongpoint defences; locations of minefields and barbed wire.

The Channel Weather Issue

General Eisenhower travelled back down to Southwick from his headquarters at Bushy Park near London on 4 June where at 2130 hours he and his service commanders assembled again for their next crucial meeting. Outside, driving rain was lashing the windows and the canvas of Montgomery's headquarters in the nearby woods (code-named SHARPENER) flapped noisily. Group Captain Stagg reported that his team had identified a ridge of high pressure developing behind the current frontal system based on vital data that had been reported by ships specially stationed in the Atlantic. His analysis was that this could provide a temporary window in the un-settled weather in the Channel and in the assault area in time for landings to take place on 6 June. Eisenhower asked how many hours he could count on for the attack. Stagg replied: 'The morning would be fair and good weather might last throughout the afternoon.' Asked for his opinion by Eisenhower, Field Marshal

Group Captain Stagg, the senior D-Day meteorologist.

Montgomery said 'I would say go!' and after a moment's thought the supreme commander gave his decision: 'OK, let's go.'

Orders were flash-signalled to the naval forces and as dusk fell on the evening of 5 June, the five ships bearing the Rangers and a LCT with the SWANs and a couple of DUKWs with stores and ammunition sufficient for immediate requirements were heading east from Portland and Weymouth with the remainder of Force O. Arriving after dark at Point Zulu off the southern tip of the Isle of Wight, here the five massive convoys bearing the assault force

Operation NEPTUNE.

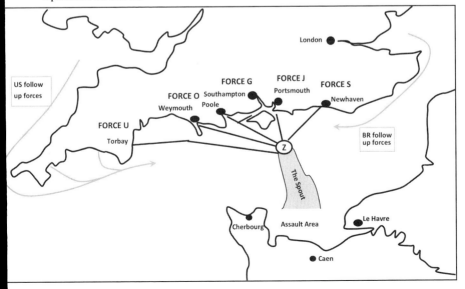

Soldiers, Sailors and Airmen of the Allied Expeditionary Force!

You are about to embark upon the Great Crusade, toward which we have striven these many months. The eyes of the world are upon you. The hopes and prayers of liberty-loving people everywhere march with you. In company with our brave Allies and brothers-in-arms on other Fronts, you will bring about the destruction of the German war machine, the elimination of Nazi tyranny over the oppressed peoples of Europe, and security for ourselves in a free world.

Your task will not be an easy one. Your enemy is well trained, well equipped and battle-hardened. He will fight savagely.

But this is the year 1944! Much has happened since the Nazi triumphs of 1940-41. The United Nations have inflicted upon the Germans great defeats, in open battle, man-to-man. Our air offensive has seriously reduced their strength in the air and their capacity to wage war on the ground. Our Home Fronts have given us an overwhelming superiority in weapons and munitions of war, and placed at our disposal great reserves of trained fighting men. The tide has turned! The free men of the world are marching together to Victory!

I have full confidence in your courage, devotion to duty and skill in battle. We will accept nothing less than full Victory!

Good Luck! And let us all beseech the blessing of Almighty God upon this great and noble undertaking.

Dwight Eisenhower

Eisenhower's D-Day message to the invasion force.

turned south into 'the Spout', five marked and mine-swept lanes. Out in the Channel for the Rangers who were by now accustomed to the cramped quarters aboard the landing ships it was still an uncomfortable night as the sea was still rough with a stiff wind.

The Germans

Some 70 miles south across the Channel the German defenders of Normandy were on a low state of alert: most commanders were on their way to a command post exercise at Le Mans, Rommel was travelling to Germany to see his wife and Hitler and the soldiers of the Atlantic Wall relaxed as best they could.

During the first few days of June the Germans had picked up indications that something was afoot, despite Allied attempts at maintaining normality. There was an increase in messenger pigeons heading north and more of the 'Personal Messages' on the BBC French station, which were in reality coded messages to the Resistance to prepare for action. On 1 June, a captured member of the Maquis (French Resistance guerrilla fighters) told his interrogators that the invasion would be in the first week of June. It is understandable that with Allied deception being so effective and a mass of intelligence coming from all sources this nugget was lost in a blizzard of information. What, however, is less understandable is that as the days went by further indicators were ignored by most but according to Ziegelmann, *Generalleutnant* Kraiss was concerned by the mounting evidence. Neither the commanders nor staff of the 716th Division to his east or the 709th on the Cotentin Peninsula shared his concerns and after seemingly months of false

A German infantryman, with helmet and rifle ready to go, waits for the invasion in the comfort of a concrete bunker.

alarms refused to bring their divisions to an enhanced state of readiness.

Even when a Fifteenth Army intelligence officer broke the codes used to communicate with the Resistance and heard the famous personal message on the BBC 'The long sobs of the Autumn Violins wound my heart with monotonous languor' (meaning that the invasion would begin in twenty-four hours) the German command was not shaken into action!

Senior German generals and their staffs were very confident in their estimate as to the specific conditions in which the Allies would launch the invasion and, as far as they were concerned, the tides were wrong for an Allied landing; i.e. it was low tide shortly before dawn. They believed that high water shortly after dawn was the prime landing time, which would allow ships to approach the coast under the cover of darkness with the bombardment and landing taking place in daylight. Of course, this tidal state also meant that the assault troops would not have to cross hundreds of yards of fire-swept beach. In addition, German weather forecasters had predicted overcast skies that would obscure the moon, which was necessary for accurate RAF bombing and airborne operations. Finally, German submarines in the Atlantic had missed the ridge of high pressure forming out in the Atlantic that Stagg and his meteorologists had spotted. In short, they believed that the tidal conditions were wrong and the weather was going to be too bad for the Allies to attempt a landing.

None the less, Kraiss put his division on alert during the night of 5/6 June. For the soldiers of the 352nd Division it was another night of exhausting watching and waiting for the invasion. The division was still on alert as word of the airborne landings on the Cotentin Peninsula and on the Caen Canal came in but incredibly

The 352nd Infantry Division's badge.

Generalleutnant **Kraiss.**

Alert again in a German artillery command post.

some German commands persisted in believing that they were raids rather than the opening act of the invasion. The Seventh Army eventually declared an alert at 0230 hours, more than two hours after the first paratroopers had jumped over Normandy.

The Passage

At 1645 hours Assault Force O-4 had weighed anchor and followed Admiral Hall's ships south-east into the sea lanes freshly swept for mines, towards the Isle of Wight. Off Saint Alban's Head they were joined by Bombardment Force C and ships carrying further elements of the 1st US Infantry Division that sailed from Poole to join the column of ships heading for Point Zulu off the southern tip of the Isle of Wight. With convoys from ports to the east and west all converging, this point was inevitably referred to as 'Piccadilly Circus'. It was now dark, and from this point it was on into the swept channels south (known as 'the Spout') through the German minefield marked by inflatable danbuoys. Several hundred mines had been cleared during the previous twenty-four hours of heavy weather.

Admiral Bertram Ramsay.

Admiral Ramsay, still at his headquarters near Portsmouth, recalled:

> There was an air of unreality during the passage of the assault forces across the Channel curiously similar to that on D-1 in HUSKY as our forces approached Sicily... [Strategic surprise was hoped for] but was by no means certain, whereas that of tactical surprise had always seemed extremely unlikely. As our forces approached the French coast without a murmur from the enemy or from their own radio, the realisation that once again complete tactical surprise had been achieved slowly dawned.

Lieutenant Colonel Rudder went onto the bridge of HMS *Prince Charles* before dawn, staring out into the dark, and the Rangers across Assault Force A tried to sleep while the ships pitched and tossed uncomfortably as they headed south in the still considerable seas. At 0328 hours, the movement changed to wallowing as the ships anchored in the transit area 10 to 12 miles out to sea.

Just after 0400 hours the Royal Navy-crewed LCAs started to be lowered from the ships' davits to the level of the deck, when a pipe over *Ben-my-Chree*'s ship's tannoy warned 'Attention on deck! United States Rangers man your boats. Good luck lads.' With the davits lowering the craft down towards the sea the Rangers did not, as many other infantrymen had, climb down wet and slippery scrambling nets that seemed designed to snag every item of military equipment and then make that calculated leap into a bucking LCA, which was being tossed around by the 5 to 6-foot swell. None the less they had to endure the drop of up to 8 feet into the water when the landing craft coxswain shouted 'Off grips' and down went the LCA.

At 0430 with the first light of dawn in the east beginning to show, the landing craft flotillas circled their mother ships before beginning the long, cold, wet and sickly journey to the shore, accompanied by the Landing Craft Tank (LCTs) with the SWANs aboard. The final element was a pair of landing craft converted to provide fire support to Assault Force O4.

Having made his decision to take command and lead the assault on Pointe du Hoc himself, Rudder in LCA 888 left the two waves

Rangers embarking in an LCA via the ship's oiling hatch.

Rangers aboard an LCA during training. The D-Day reality of poor weather and darkness was very different.

bearing Ranger Force C to join Ranger Force A which had completed disembarkation from *Ben-my-Chree*. Lieutenant Colonel Rudder had not told General Huebner of his change of plan.

The landing craft flotillas had only been under way for a short while before the rough sea took its first casualty. Some 8 miles from shore LCA 860 with Captain Slater's headquarters and a platoon of Company D (Ranger Force A) shipped so much water that she foundered and sank. All were, however, picked up and eventually re-joined the 2nd Rangers. Not so lucky were the overloaded supply LCAs. The first, LCA 914, was lost with all hands except one Ranger and the second only survived by dumping overboard the packs belonging to Companies D and E.

The rest of the craft survived this part of the journey but in almost every case waves breaking over the low freeboard of the LCAs required the Rangers to assist the pumps by bailing out with their helmets. While the Rangers were distracted from seasickness by bailing, everything aboard the LCAs was soaked including the hemp ropes attached to the rocket grapples.

Most of the sectionalized Commando ladders that had been strapped to the topsides of the LCAs were washed off by the waves and lost overboard during the journey to the shore.

The Navigation Error

The landing craft flotilla bearing the Rangers was led on the two-hour journey to the coast of Normandy by a 112-foot long Fairmile Motor Launch (ML) attached from the 11th ML Flotilla. ML 304, commanded by Lieutenant Colin Beevor, RNVR was armed with a 3-pounder gun on the forward deck, one twin and a single 20mm Oerlikon, plus two machine guns. For his primary role of navigating the Rangers to Pointe du Hoc he had two aids. The first was radar that would pick up the cliffs as he headed inshore giving him distance if not an accurate profile of the coastline ahead of him. The second was the QH2 radio-based system that read a series of intersecting beams that had been propagated across the invasion area. All was well until both of these systems failed at 0530 hours, with it later being established that there had been a power failure in the vital circuits aboard ML 304 due to a blown fuse!

The result was that Lieutenant Beevor now had to resort to traditional navigation methods in a difficult situation. It was still around dawn and difficult to pick out landmarks and the coast was in any case wreathed in smoke from the aerial bombing and naval gunfire, plus a current was running far more strongly to the east than expected. It had also been expected to easily identify the cliff-top battery from the flashes of the 150mm guns but of these there were none. Consequently, the Provisional Ranger Group was heading towards Pointe de la Percée, some 3 miles east of Pointe du Hoc. The Hunt-class destroyer HMS *Talybont*, however, had correctly identified Pointe du Hoc from the detonation of USS *Texas*'s 14-inch shells.

A Fairmile B of the same type as ML 304.

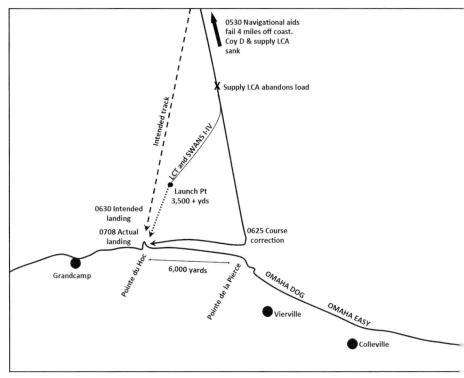

The navigational error.

Much covert study of the beaches, commensurate with maintaining security, had revealed the expected tidal pattern. Naval sources record: 'It was known that with a rising tide (low tide on 6 June was at 0525), a strong current ran laterally eastward along OMAHA Beach, reaching a maximum velocity of nearly 2.7 knots at 5 miles offshore; strong winds might increase its average velocity.'

The strength, however, of the easterly current off Pointe du Hoc and OMAHA Beach on D-Day came as a surprise and no doubt contributed to Lieutenant Beevor's navigational problems. An indication of just how strongly the current was running in the area is afforded by a report from USS *Satterlee* that she 'had to steer 20 to 30 degrees "up current" to maintain her position in the firing line.'

Another factor in the navigational error was that the bombing since 15 April had so altered the appearance of the cliff that had been appearing out of the gloom that Lieutenant Beevor had not been able to recognize Pointe du Hoc from the montage of oblique air photos taken by the Allied photo reconnaissance squadrons from seaward, often flying just above the waves.

The German Defenders and the Bombardment

Obergrenadier Wagner was on the cliffs at the western end of OMAHA Beach in the area of Wn 72, adjacent to Company C, the 2nd Rangers' objective:

> I was on guard in my position, which was near Vierville. It was the last hour of duty for me when dawn arrived. My eyes hurt from the strain. I was tired, cold and hungry. Soon our relief would be here. I pushed aside the machine gun that I was resting my chin on in order to take another look with the binoculars. I had never been in battle before so I was pretty nervous. I was afraid to see anything, for two reasons. One, because if I sounded the alarm and it was nothing my friends would be mad at me for disturbing their precious sleep, and two, if it was real I was worried that I might freeze up stiff. With thoughts like these running through my mind I peered out the view slit onto the water. Suddenly I saw something out there. In the darkness, I wasn't sure what kind of craft it was but it was heading straight at us.

The air and naval bombardment was designed to downgrade German defences and defenders, leaving them stunned as the Allies stormed ashore. According to RAF historian John Terraine: 'On the night of 5/6 June 1,056 Lancasters, Halifaxes and Mosquitos set out to drop 5,267 tons of bombs on ten coastal batteries forming part of the Atlantic Wall defences in which Field Marshal Rommel hoped to be able to resist and defeat the Allied landings.'

At Pointe du Hoc, the bombing started the previous evening with a raid by B-24 Liberators of the Second Bombardment Division of the Eighth US Air Force starting at 2224 hours and then RAF Bomber Command joined the battle: 114 of the 124 aircraft tasked to raid Pointe du Hoc dropped 1,066 1,000lb bombs between 0446 and 0503 hours.

The pre-dawn attack by the RAF was followed at 0550 (nautical twilight) by forty minutes of naval gunfire by the US, British and French ships of Bombardment Force C. USS *Texas* fired 226 14-inch rounds, which combined with the bombing left the battery very heavily cratered as can be seen today. Admiral Hall's Western Task Force report described the bombardment's effect:

> Pre-H-hour air bombardment and naval gunfire completely disrupted communications and communication trenches, badly

Lancaster bombers were in action over Normandy from dusk until just before dawn.

damaged or destroyed open positions, and breached perimeter wire and mine bands [fields]. No serious damage was observed on underground shelters, O.P. or finished casemates which were constructed of reinforced concrete, despite many hits.

On OMAHA Beach where Ranger Forces B and C were to land a post-dawn bombing run by the USAAF failed largely because of smoke and dust with only a few bombs landing anywhere near the target. More than 100 aircraft returned to their stations in England with their load of ordnance. Meanwhile, at 0625 hours, twenty

USS *Texas* in action on D-Day.

minutes late, seventeen B-26 Marauders struck at Pointe du Hoc but most of their bombs also fell harmlessly inland. A total of 698 tons of bombs was dropped on Pointe du Hoc during the night of 5/6 June 1944 and prior to H-hour.

The Final Run-In

It wasn't until daylight that Rudder, aboard an LCA only a couple of feet above the waterline and less than a mile off the coast, realized that a navigational error had been made. As the distance decreased and the light improved, it was possible to discern features in what had been a uniformly dark wall of cliffs. He spoke to the naval officer of the 501st Assault Flotilla pointing out the error but to no avail. Exasperated, Rudder ordered the coxswain: 'Godammit, turn right.' Rudder subsequently wrote: 'We had to take control; of the landing craft, ourselves and guide them to the proper landing area.' Using semaphore flags the naval officer signalled his craft to conform to his movement and steer to starboard, into the current. It was now, with 3 miles to regain, impossible for Ranger Force A to meet its 0630 H-hour and attack the Pointe du Hoc guns.

At 0630 hours, with the first landings, radio silence was lifted and every radio net had come to life on the crowded analogue frequencies. The more powerful sets of the navy's ships blotted out the smaller crafts' radios and the even less powerful manpack versions, which had suffered a soaking in the smaller craft. The result was that hardly anyone could communicate in the run-in to OMAHA Beach; so much so that German jamming efforts were barely necessary! These communication problems extended to the LCAs of Ranger Force A. Consequently, when Lieutenant Colonel Rudder tried to inform Lieutenant Colonel Schneider and the bulk of the Ranger Group of the navigational error and delay, he could not get through.

During the slow transit to the west with the craft now almost beam on to the waves bailing resumed and the enemy section positions along the clifftop took the opportunity to engage the nine surviving landing craft at long range. Several Rangers were hit and one of the four SWANs was holed by 20mm fire and sunk.

Meanwhile, the supporting destroyers had noted the misdirection of the flotilla and the fact that they were under fire as they transited west. *American Forces in Action* recorded:

Hunt-class destroyer HMS *Talybont*.

As the Rangers corrected course and came under fire from the cliff positions, the *Talybont* closed range and for 15 minutes (0645–0700) raked enemy firing positions with 4-inch and 2-pounder shells. Meantime, the US destroyer *Satterlee*, 2,500 yards from Pointe du Hoe [*sic*], could see enemy troops assembling on the cliff, and opened with main battery and machine-gun fire.

As the Rangers approached Pointe du Hoc, little did they know that there was a two-man reception party waiting for them that had been watching earnestly as the landing craft headed west towards them. They were the sole survivors of a Dakota bearing eighteen men of Company I of the 3rd 506th Parachute Infantry that had been hit by anti-aircraft fire.

Chapter Five

Ranger Force B at OMAHA Beach

Captain Goranson's Company C, 2nd Rangers had a mission to land on CHARLIE Sector, get across the beach, scale the cliffs and clear Wn 73 whose plunging fire could rake up to half of OMAHA Beach from west to east. They disembarked from HMS *Prince Charles* into two LCAs for the long run-in to the beach below the cliffs rising at the western end of OMAHA.

Before giving an account of Ranger Force B's actions, it is necessary to put their plan and action firmly in context of that of Colonel Canham's 116th US Infantry Regiment that was to land on the western portion of OMAHA Beach adjacent to Company C.

Preceded by a run-in shoot delivered by the escorting destroyers and field artillery pieces firing from the craft, all designed to 'drench' the beach with fire, thirty-two Duplex Drive (DD) Shermans of the 743rd Tank Battalion would land at H minus 5 minutes (H-5). Having swum from 6,000 yards out to sea, once on the beach, the standard A4 Shermans were to drop their screens and

The view down on OMAHA Beach from Wn 73.

engage German defences with direct fire, thus providing cover for the four infantry companies that would land at H+1. Company C along with elements of the Special Engineer Task Force would land at H+3, with the Rangers landing on CHARLIE Sector to the east See table on p. 66 of the Vierville draw, which was known as DOG 1. Subsequent waves, predominantly of infantry and engineers, would land at H+30, H+40, H+50 and H+57. After that, the build-up of men and equipment, artillery and other combat support and combat service support units would be landed. If it were to become necessary to deliver Lieutenant Colonel Schneider's Ranger Force C to OMAHA Beach, they would be inserted in the waves landing on DOG GREEN sector at H+60, H+65 and H+70.

At 0430 hours Ranger Force B disembarked from HMS *Prince Charles* into two LCAs (Nos 418 and 1038) of the 504th Assault Flotilla and joined Assault Group O-2, forming up in the long columns of landing craft heading for the western portion of OMAHA Beach. Their place was just behind Company A of the 116th Infantry. As with Ranger Force A, it was to be a long, cold and wet run-in to the beach. Lieutenant Salmon, who was standing in the bows, recalled optimistically thinking as his LCA closed to within half a mile of the beach: 'Maybe the Jerries have abandoned their coastal defences to make their stand further inland.' How wrong one can be!

The Landing on DOG GREEN

Nowhere on D-Day was the military maxim that 'No plan survives contact with the enemy' more appropriate than on OMAHA Beach. It was not only Ranger Force A who were having difficulties with the easterly flowing current, as much of Assault Force O was set to the left and landed to the east of their designated spot. On the right, however, B Company, 743rd Tank Battalion, A Company of the 116th Infantry and Ranger Force B had the landmarks of the end of the beach and the rising cliffs to help them touch down accurately but effectively isolated. The landing craft bearing Company G who should have been landing on DOG WHITE touched down over 1,000 yards to the east on EASY GREEN (Les Moulins). F and G companies were also set to the west. Consequently, the full fury of the five *Widerstandsnest* at the western end of the beach could be concentrated on just three sub-units on the broad expanse of OMAHA Beach.

The DOG GREEN 'killing area' from Wn 73.

Scheduled to land just before 0630 hours, the 743rd Tank Battalion was in potential difficulties when their LCT reached the launching-point, where 6ft waves were dashing against its grey sides. The sea was far too rough to launch the 35-ton Duplex Drive (commonly known as 'Donald Duck') amphibious tanks supported only by their flimsy canvas screens. The LCTs' skippers with Company B aboard decided to bring the tanks in as close as they dared and launched the DDs, which with their screens up waded rather than swam ashore. The US history records: 'The LCT carrying the company commander was sunk just off shore, and four other officers were killed or wounded, leaving one lieutenant in Company B. Eight of that company's sixteen tanks landed and started to fire from the water's edge on enemy positions.'

The DDs of Company B, coming in directly in face of the *Widerstandsnest* covering the Vierville draw, suffered heavily from the enemy's casemated anti-tank and artillery fire, which had all survived the bombardment. The US history, however, records that 'The tanks of Companies C and A touched down to the east at well-spaced intervals and without initial losses.'

101

A DD tank with its screen down.

A rear view of a DD tank with its screen erected and Duplex Drive propellers visible.

The wisdom of the young naval officers in landing the DDs of the 743rd Tank Battalion at wading depth is demonstrated by the fate of the 741st who, landing on the eastern portion of the beach, lost virtually all their tanks while still thousands of yards from their sector of the beach.

With Company B's DD tanks fighting for their own survival among the beach obstacles, the infantry of Company A were landing behind schedule at H+6 on DOG GREEN from six Landing Craft Vehicle and Personnel (LCVPs), each carrying approximately thirty-two men. With every German weapon from bluff, cliff and at the bottom of the draw they came

> under fire as they passed within a quarter-mile of the shore, the infantry met their worst experiences of the day and suffered their heaviest casualties just after touchdown. Small arms fire, mortars, and artillery concentrated on the landing area, but the worst hazard was produced by converging fires from automatic weapons. Survivors from some craft report hearing the fire beat on the ramps before they were lowered, and then seeing the hail of bullets whip the surf just in front of the lowered ramps. Some men dove under water or went over the sides to escape the beating zone of the machine guns. Stiff, weakened from seasickness, and often heavily loaded, the debarking troops had little chance of moving fast in water that was knee deep or higher, and their progress was made more difficult by uneven footing in the runnels crossing the tidal flat. Many men were exhausted before they reached shore, where they faced 200 yards or more of open sand to cross before reaching cover at the sea wall or shingle bank. Most men who reached that cover made it by walking, and under increasing enemy fire. Troops who stopped to organize, rest, or take shelter behind obstacles or tanks merely prolonged their difficulties and suffered heavier losses.

As far as Company A of the 116th was concerned, one of their landing craft foundered about 1,000 yards off shore. The Rangers to their right and too far to the rear to help saw men jumping overboard and being dragged down by their heavy loads. At H+6 minutes the five remaining craft grounded in 4 feet of water about 30 yards short of the most seaward obstacles. The *American Forces in Action* monograph described the disembarkation:

TYPICAL GUN EMPLACEMENTS

TURRET MOUNT, 240-280 MM
ILLUSTRATED BY 265267

CASEMATE, 105-150 MM
ILLUSTRATED BY 360022

EMPLACEMENT WITH CONC SHELT, 130-180MM
ILLUSTRATED BY 240264

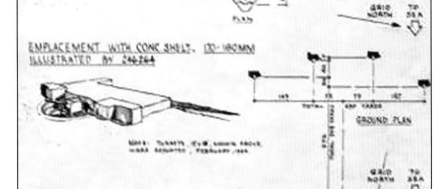

OPEN, 155 MM HOWITZER
ILLUSTRATED BY 53398

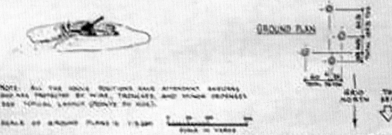

NOTE: ALL THE ABOVE POSITIONS HAVE ATTENDANT SHELTERS
AND ARE PROTECTED BY WIRE, TRENCHES, AND MINOR DEFENSES
SEE TYPICAL LAYOUT (ABOVE IN RED).

SCALE OF GROUND PLANS 1:7500

Starting off the craft in three files, center file first and the flank files peeling right and left, the men were enveloped in accurate and intense fire from automatic weapons. Order was quickly lost as the troops attempted to dive under water or dropped over the sides into surf over their heads.

Mortar rounds scored four hits on one of the landing craft, which 'disintegrated'. Men were falling, staining the surf red with their blood as they made their way to the beach, and when the survivors got there many found the fire too intense and headed back into the dubious cover of the sea. As the tide rose around them others took refuge behind the German beach obstacles. The survivors of the 180 men who landed with Company A could not establish a firing line; it was a matter of individual survival. The account continued:

> In short order, every officer of the company, including Capt. Taylor N. Fellers, was a casualty, and most of the sergeants were killed or wounded. The leaderless men gave up any attempt to move forward and confined their efforts to saving the wounded, many of whom drowned in the rising tide. Some troops were later able to make the sea wall by staying in the edge of the water and going up the beach with the tide.

Within fifteen minutes of landing, Company A was virtually destroyed by concentrated enemy fire and most of the tanks that had reached the shore were knocked out. Landing 500 yards to the right on CHARLIE Sector, the Rangers of Captain Goranson's Company C would be very much on their own.

One of the classic OMAHA Beach images taken by Robert Cappa.

Ranger Force B

The two LCAs, with the sixty-three men of Company C aboard, had a low freeboard and made slower progress than the American LCPVs as they approached the defended shore of Hitler's vaunted Atlantic Wall. While there had been plenty of fire and, latterly, aircraft passing overhead towards the enemy defences, there was very little fire and none that had been noticed by Company C aimed at them. When, however, they were just hundreds of yards from the beach, Sergeant Golas ducked down into the LCA, reporting 'Gee fellows, they're shooting back at us!'

Captain Goranson and his Rangers touched down some time after Company A, possibly as much as nine minutes later at H+15, but they landed accurately beneath the clifftop position of Wn 73. They were greeted with the same deluge of fire from the defenders, with Captain Goranson's craft being hit at the cost of a dozen men and severely shaking others. Another craft was sunk by a pair of direct hits from mortars, probably from the three pits at Wn 73.

According to their report: 'An enemy machine gun ranged in on the ramps of the second LCA and hit Rangers as they debarked.' The survivors from this landing craft, with the 'Get off the beach' credo of the Commandos and Rangers ringing in their ears, dashed across 250 yards of horribly open fire-swept beach to the base of

Captain Ralph Goranson, commander of Ranger Group A.

106

British LCAs had a narrow exit and ramp; only one Ranger could disembark at a time.

the cliff. Here, too exhausted to move, the Rangers spent several minutes counting heads and reorganizing themselves, all the while sheltering among the boulders at the bottom of the cliff from mortar and machine-gun fire from left and right. 'Potato-masher' grenades were also being thrown down from the cliffs above and from the area of Fortified House.

By this time they had suffered thirty-five casualties: in the landing craft, during their disembarkation and their headlong dash across the beach. Among them was the company radio operator, Captain Goranson's link to the 116th Infantry. Only twenty-eight Rangers and two survivors of Company A, 116th Infantry, Privates Lovejoy and Shefer, were available for the attack on Wn 73.

While the reorganization was being completed, Captain Goranson sent three Rangers under Lieutenant Moody west along the foot of the cliff to find a route up the 100ft-high wall of rock and mudstone. The cliff here was not as vertical as it was at Pointe du Hoc and the Rangers were able to find a narrow but still steep gully that was climbable, some 300 yards to the west. Using his Commando knives for a hand-hold on the looser muddy sections, Lieutenant Moody was able to get up the cleft. He took with him four toggle ropes that he looped together and secured on a stake in the dummy minefield on the top of the cliff. This enabled his comrades to easily scale the loose upper section. Moody and his men were almost certainly the first Americans up from OMAHA Beach onto the high ground.

107

Ranger Force C, OMAHA Beach.

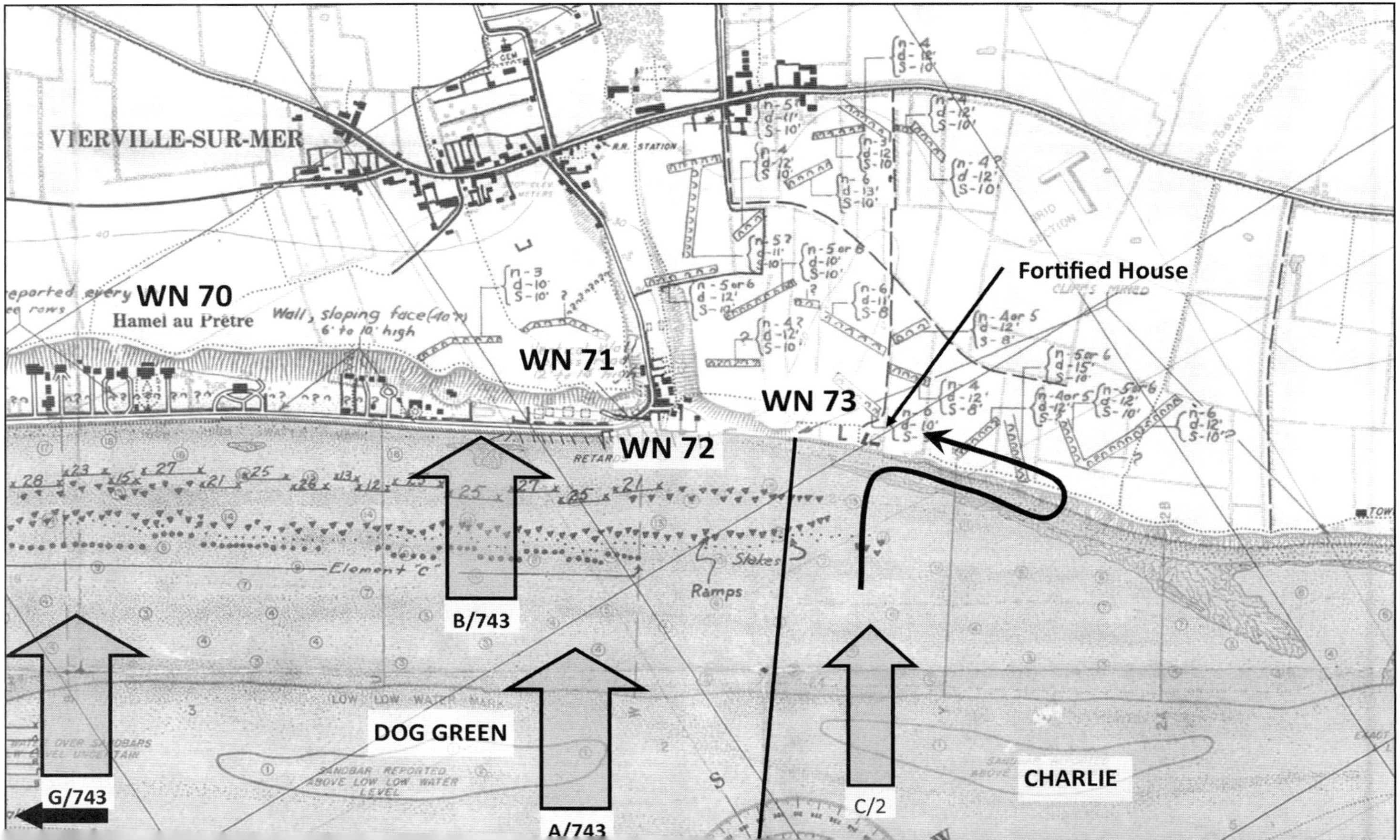

Fortified House

CHARLIE

C/2

WN 73

WN 72

WN 71

A/743

DOG GREEN

B/743

G/743

VIERVILLE-SUR-MER

WN 70

Hamel au Prêtre

Wall, sloping face (40")
6' to 10' high

They had emerged on top of the cliff to the west of the dip in the cliff occupied by Fortified House and Wn 73 just beyond it. Lieutenant Moody and Private Otto edged their way towards the German positions with Sergeant Belcher giving covering fire, until they reached a point from where they could shout details of the route up the cliff to the rest of the company on the beach below. With more ropes rigged, the Rangers were quickly up the cliff by 0730 hours and formed into a tight defensive beachhead. Captain Goranson reinforced Lieutenant Moody to make his strength up to a third of the remaining company and sent him forward to clear Fortified House. They quickly gained a foothold in the German defences in the dip and house, killing a German officer in the process:

> When the house was reached, the Rangers found just beyond it lay a German strongpoint [Wn 73] consisting of a maze of dugouts and trenches, including machine-gun emplacements and mortar positions. Captain Goranson put men in an abandoned trench just west of the house and started to feel out the enemy positions on the other side.

By now the Germans were only too well aware of the Rangers' presence on the clifftop near Wn 73 and with the situation under control on the beach in front of Wn 71 and 72 were able to reinforce and counter-attack the Rangers, repeatedly driving them back out of the Wn 73 trenches. At this stage of the battle, even though he was exacting a heavy price on the German counter-attackers, Captain Goranson simply lacked the men and consequently the combat power to take and hold the clifftop defences.

Meanwhile, the landing craft of the second wave with Company B of the 116th Infantry aboard, due to touch down at 0700 hrs (H+30), failed to pick up landmarks and with the plan having clearly miscarried, their six craft became badly scattered, beaching on a frontage of nearly 1,500 yards astride DOG GREEN. 'The craft which touched down on or near DOG GREEN came under the same destructive fire which had wrecked Company A and the remnants of the boat sections mingled with those of Company A in an effort for survival at the water's edge.'

The Rangers, however, spotted one of Company B's landing craft beaching on CHARLIE Sector almost directly below. Captain Goranson promptly sent a Ranger down the cliff to get them to come and support him. Relieved to be off the beach, the section of

A visitor standing in one of the Wn 73 trenches overlooking DOG and CHARLIE.

about ten former National Guardsmen of the 29th Infantry Division was soon making its way up the cliff to the Ranger beachhead.

In the meantime, Lieutenant Moody had been joined in the area to the west of Fortified House by Lieutenant Salmon. In attempting to see more clearly the lie of the enemy defences ahead of them, Lieutenant Moody, rising up to get a better view, received a shot to the head and fell dead into the shell-hole in which the pair of officers had been sheltering. Lieutenant Salmon, now reinforced by Rangers relieved in the clifftop beachhead by soldiers of Company B, advanced again towards and into Wn 73. This time their advance took them into the trenches and bunkers on the crest, where they started to go through the emplacements with grenades and bursts of fire from submachine guns and rifles. 'Enemy reinforcements kept coming up along communication trenches from the Vierville draw, and the Ranger parties were not quite able to clean out the system of trenches and dugouts.'

Eventually, with a firm toe-hold in cleared trenches and bunkers on the crest, the Rangers were now able to look down on the carnage on OMAHA Beach below. In reaching this point behind some of the cliff-edge bunkers the Rangers had made those further down the slope untenable and the enfilading fire onto the beach that had been so destructive earlier on was gradually brought under control. Later almost seventy bodies of German soldiers were collected from the area of Wn 73, most of them killed in action with Ranger Force B. However, now isolated, under persistent small-arms fire from inland and across the draw, with no radio communications and with insufficient strength to push on, all Captain Goranson could do was to hold on to his not insignificant gains. It was obvious then than that things were not going well and Goranson must have been a very worried man, expecting a heavy German counter-attack at any time.

During this period the German pressure mounted and the Rangers received the welcome help of the US navy. On one occasion, an American fire support craft opened up with her 20mm cannon on an approaching enemy force that the Rangers had not seen. With the fire cracking past just overhead, the Rangers were alarmed but the attack had been broken up before it came into contact. Inevitably, with smoke from the burning scrub and the bursting of shells billowing around the clifftop, there were incidents of fratricide but the Rangers were now occupying the bunkers in which the enemy had successfully sheltered during the pre-landing bombardment. Consequently there were only minor injuries when one of the destroyers opened fire on the part of the cliff held by the Rangers.

During the morning and afternoon, as the course of the battle on the beaches and bluffs was turning in favour of the Americans, the Rangers were able to push forward, driving the Germans out of

The gun from the square-mouthed casemate in Wn 73 enfilading the length of OMAHA has been attributed a wide variety of calibres but based on the contemporary photograph and the muzzle brake set in the sea wall it is 100/105mm.

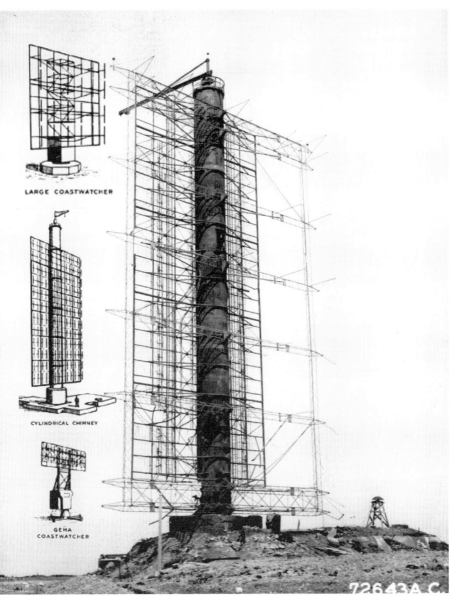

The Germans deployed a variety of radars as a part of the Atlantic Wall. Seen here is a photograph of the Wassermann S and sketches from the Neptune Monograph.

trenches and the murder holes overlooking the Vierville draw. DOG 1 was open!

Later in the day Company C was able to make its way a mile west along the cliffs but when they arrived at Wn 74 (Pointe et Raz de la

Percée) they found that it had been very badly smashed up by the fire of the light cruiser HMS *Glasgow*'s twelve 6in guns. After an hour or so of the landings she was able to neutralize the German gunners in Wn 74 and keep them neutralized.

On the evening of D-Day, the now small group of Rangers still with Captain Goranson moved on to Vierville where they joined up with Ranger Force C and took part in the defence of the OMAHA bridgehead that night.

Captain Goranson and Company C, following a shocking landing during which they lost 40 per cent of their already slim strength of a Ranger company in a matter of minutes, had pressed on with their mission, scaling the cliffs and attacking fixed defences when many would have thought discretion the better part of valour. Albeit with the focus of the landings shifting further east along OMAHA Beach, Company C and its small reinforcement from Company B, 116th Infantry had made a significant contribution to overcoming resistance at the western end of the beach. Infantry trenches, several machine-gun nests, three mortar positions and an artillery piece had been accounted for, greatly reducing the effectiveness of the Germans' interlocking and overlapping arcs of fire covering the Vierville draw and the slopes up to Wn 70 and 71.

Chapter Six

Pointe du Hoc: Escalade and Assault

The fortifications at Pointe du Hoe [*sic*] had been under heavy
fire . . . However, this fire had been lifted according to schedule
and when the Rangers landed. . .the Germans had filtered back
into the fortifications and were waiting for them with machine
guns, mortars, rifles and hand grenades. . . . As the Rangers
landed they found themselves pinned under the cliffs and were
being rapidly cut to pieces.

American Forces in Action

Due to a power failure aboard ML 304, Ranger Force A had
headed to Pointe de la Percée and had not realized the error until
just before their planned H-hour of 0630 when they were only
1,000 yards off the coast of Normandy. According to Lieutenant
Beevor aboard ML 304 in his 'report on proceedings' the SWANs
had already been unloaded: 'At 4,000 yards the LCT was instructed
to stop and the "Ducks" were launched.'

As the coxswains of the nine LCAs, the single surviving supply
craft and the fire support vessels (LCS) put their helms to starboard, they headed in double column into the strong east-flowing
current. Being within range of both enemy machine guns and
20mm cannon, the flotilla came under fire from the cliffs. Lieutenant Commander Baines watched the slow move east from the
bridge of HMS *Talybont* and later wrote in the ship's log 'Their
course from Pte de la Percée along the shore to Pte du Hoc was
suicidal.' Being low in the water and half a mile from the coast,
casualties aboard the LCAs were, however, light but it was the first
time under fire for Rudder and most of the Rangers.

Meanwhile, disembarking from their LCTs that had navigated to
the correct off-loading point within 4,000 yards of the Pointe,
SWAN II was quickly lost to 20mm fire from the area of the radar
station. The accompanying Landing Craft Support (LCS) 91 and
102 replied with suppressive fire from Oerlikons and .50 calibre
machine guns.

As the flotilla approached, the clouds of smoke from the naval
bombardment that had wreathed the clifftop started to clear once
fire was lifted from the battery, but it was already well past the time

The 20mm *Flakvierling* (FlaK) 38 of the type commonly used in the Atlantic Wall.

they should have landed and secured the guns. Rudder realized that it would take even longer to swing out to seaward and approach the Pointe from the north and land together astride the headland as planned. Consequently, a change was signalled to the other craft to come into line abreast of Rudder's LCA, with the two surviving LCAs from Company D slotting in-between Companies E and F for a landing on the eastern face of the Pointe rather than on the western side.

Conforming to the movements of Rudder's craft, a ragged line was formed as the craft approached the narrow beach at the foot of the cliffs, varying in width from 10 to 30 yards. With *Talybont* having checked firing, the approach and landing was covered by

With the heavy powered ladder aboard, the SWAN sat even lower in the water than a standard DUKW.

the fire of the two LCSs and ML 304. Lieutenant Beevor's report continued:

> The landing was effected without opposition [difficult to see as he was out to sea] and at this point the top of the cliff became clearly visible. The smoke had cleared away and several huts and concrete emplacements could be observed. While the landing was in progress, I engaged these targets with 3 Pdr and 20mm Oerlikon fire at ranges from 700–1,000 yards. 20 rounds of 3 Pdr F.S. were fired into the huts and emplacements and 1,000 rounds of Oerlikon were used to spray the top of the cliff until the ascent was completed. A few figures were discerned moving about on the top of the cliff, but these were fired on and appeared to take cover.

None the less, the enemy infantry from III/726 *Infanterie-Regiment* had been given time to recover from the effects of USS *Texas*'s bombardment which ended at 0620 hours and were no longer shocked and dazed as they were driven out of the bunkers and the shelter of 6 feet of concrete into what was left of their trenches. *Talybont* had engaged the Pointe between 0645 and 0700 hours but there was a big difference between her four 4in guns and *Texas*'s ten 14in and twelve 5in guns. USS *Satterlee* was also in action in the area further out to sea where she could see Germans moving around the battery site and engaged with her 5in guns, giving covering fire during the landing along with ML 304 as already described. Once on the beach this fire, according to Lieutenant Colonel Rudder, 'scared the living hell out of me' as rock and concrete thrown up by the detonating shells rained down on the Rangers. Without the fire from US and British naval vessels, it is difficult to see how Rudder and his men could have succeeded.

The Beach Landing

The landing craft approached the beach in a ragged line as the LCAs at the rear of the column struggled to deploy. They came in obliquely from the east on a frontage of around 500 yards, with the craft of Company E being displaced to the east by Company D. First to touch down was LCA 888 with the 2nd Rangers' signals officer Lieutenant Eikner, a part of Rudder's headquarters, noting that it was 0708 hours, some thirty-eight minutes late. The landing craft coxswains reported that the remainder of the LCAs touched down within the next three or four minutes.

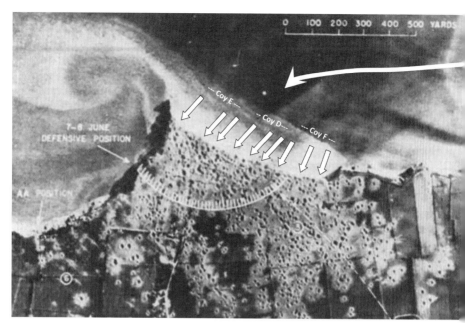

The landing.

First out was Rudder onto a beach that was a mess of fallen rock and larger boulders blown down during the bombing and bombardment, plus large flooded craters in the clay rock that made up the under-layer of the beach. These had been made by bombs or shells that had fallen short of their target and the beach was not at all like those on which they had trained in England. Most of the LCAs came to rest just short of the beach and many Rangers stepping off the ramps found themselves plunging into deep submerged shell-holes and, heavily laden, they struggled to regain the surface and to climb the slippery clay sides onto the beach. Not only was the arrival of the landing craft staggered but with only one man able to disembark from an LCA at a time, along with the state of the beach, the landing was certainly not a concerted rush to the foot of the cliff. The US historian noted: 'The craters were to handicap the unloading of men and supplies and were to render the DUKWs useless after landing, for these craft were nowhere able to cross the sand and get close enough to the cliff to reach it with their extension ladders.'

While they were disembarking and making their way across the beach, the Rangers were under fire from machine guns and riflemen around the Pointe and from German positions to the east of the battery. Not only that, from above grenades were being thrown

The beach covered in fallen rock and shell-holes.

down by the defending infantry in quantity. This fire was effective but fortunately, as these were predominantly blast grenades and because many fell into crevices between boulders or shell-holes, they were not as effective as they could have been. Two men from LCA 862 were wounded by grenades. Despite naval gunfire support, most boats reported seeing enemy active above them and the Rangers took shots at what were inevitably fleeting targets. One of Company E's LCAs that had grounded about 25 yards from the beach saw 'Three or four Germans standing on the cliff edge, shooting down at the craft. Rangers near the stern took these enemy under fire and drove them out of sight.'

Landing from the same LCA as Rudder, 'Sergeant Boggetto shot one German off the edge with a BAR [Browning Automatic Rifle], the others disappeared.'

As the landing craft came into the beach, from a distance of 35 yards out they each started to fire their six large rocket-powered grapples in series with plain ropes followed by the heavier toggle ropes and finally the lightweight rope ladders. Of the fifty-four

119

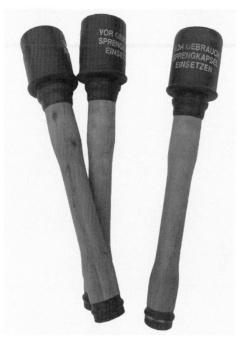

German stick grenades.   A grapple.

rockets available on the nine LCAs, few got to the top and provided viable routes off the beach: some failed to ignite, others with
the hemp rope soaked were too heavy to reach the clifftop, while of
those that did some did not hold in the loose soil thrown up by the
bombing and bombardment and yet more were cut or dislodged by
the German infantrymen.

The US historian recorded that in the case of the rockets on
LCA 861 (Company E): 'All the ropes fell short of the cliff edge, as
a result of being thoroughly soaked. In some cases, not more than
half the length of rope or ladder was lifted from the containing
box.' Aboard LCA 862 from the same company that touched down
about 100 yards to the left, 'One plain and two toggle ropes reached
the top, but one toggle rope pulled out.'

Meanwhile, once ashore and set up, Lieutenant Eikner, Lieutenant Colonel Rudder's signals officer, got into cover along with the
rest of Rudder's headquarters in a shallow cave at the bottom of
the cliff. From here he tried to send the signal that Ranger Force A
had landed beneath Pointe du Hoc. Having stripped the water-
proofing and coaxed the delicate valve-technology radio set into
life, by his own estimation at 0725 hours he sent the code-word
'CROWBAR', primarily aimed at Ranger Force C, that they had

landed but by that time Lieutenant Colonel Schneider and his Rangers from the 2nd and 5th battalions were already steering towards OMAHA Beach. Exactly which stations aboard ship and landing craft received Eikner's signals is not clear but suffice to say that Schneider was already committed and if they heard anything from Ranger Force A it was 'unworkable'.

The Cliff Assault

For the assault force to be able to climb the ropes quickly and reach the guns on the clifftop, speed was essential for the escalade phase. Consequently, the Rangers were lightly equipped 'for shock action of limited duration, with a minimum load of supplies and weapons.' Dressed in the lighter weight herringbone denim uniform, the Rangers all wore light assault scales of web equipment, ammunition, two grenades and a high-energy D-bar ration. Most members of Ranger Force A carried the standard hard-hitting M-1 rifle but a few of those who were going to be first up the ropes carried pistols or carbines.

Each landing-craft load of Rangers faced its own particular challenge depending on the success of the rocket grapples fired from their LCAs, the profile of the cliff in front of them and how exposed they were to enemy fire. Those that had viable ropes fired from the LCA went for them. It will be recalled that LCA 862 had two secure ropes: 'Ranger Aguzzi, Lieutenant Leagans and Staff Sergeant Cleaves went up the two remaining ropes, arrived at the top almost together, and fell into a convenient shell hole just beyond the edge.'

Even if the grapples held securely, it wasn't a guaranteed way up. Company D from LCA 668 landed in the central area and had two plain ropes and a toggle on the clifftop. 'Sergeant Lomell put his best climber on the toggle ... All ropes were on an overhang, and only the toggle line proved practicable.' After days of bad weather and with the Rangers soaked, another problem emerged and that was that the plain ropes quickly became covered in slippery clay mud, adding to the difficulty and in some cases the impossibility of climbing them after the passage up the cliff by a couple of men. Another Company D team aboard LCA 858 was luckier with a single plain rope: 'They could get footholds in the cliff face, and a big crater reduced the steepness of the climb near the top. The group was up within fifteen minutes.'

German infantry weapons.

The Rangers aboard those LCAs that had not successfully
launched their rockets had to rely on their lighter portable rockets.
In the case of Company E,

> the hand-rockets were carried ashore, and the first one was
> fired at 15 yards from the cliff. It went over the top and caught.
> Pfc. Harry W. Roberts started up the hand-line, bracing his
> feet against the 80-degree slope. He made about 25 feet; the
> rope slipped or was cut, and Roberts slithered down. The
> second rocket was fired and the grapnel caught. Roberts went
> up again, made the top (he estimated his climbing time at
> 40 seconds), and pulled into a small cratered niche just under
> the edge. As he arrived, the rope was cut. Roberts tied it to a
> picket. This pulled out under the weight of the next man, and
> the rope fell off the cliff, marooning Roberts.

A light rocket grapple being fired during training.

Lieutenant Arman had realized that the heavier ropes of the craft-mounted rockets 'had no chance' of reaching the cliff from the edge of the sea. So, with ten minutes of heavy manhandling, four of his LCA's rockets 'together with the boxes carrying toggle ropes and ladders, were taken out on to the sand.' However, when the rockets were set up on the beach, the firing wire connection was found to be missing. Sergeant Cripps selflessly fired the rockets in turn by touching the short connection, 3 feet from the rocket base, with his 'hot-box':

> Each time, the flashback blinded Cripps and blew sand and mud all over him. The other Rangers saw him clean his eyes, shake his head, and go after the next rocket: 'He was the hell-of-a-looking mess.' But all the ropes went up, and made it possible for the party to make the top. Sergeant Petty and

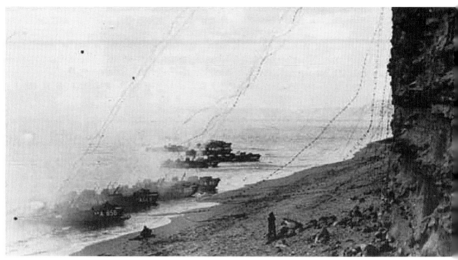

Craft-mounted rocket grapples in use during training at Burton Bradstock.

some other expert climbers had already tried the plain rope and failed; it was on a straight fall, requiring hand-over-hand work with no footholds possible, and the men had trouble with their muddy hands and clothes on the wet rope.

Other teams found that the ramps of rubble blown off the upper section of the cliff could be climbed and that there was only a relatively short section of steep cliff to be climbed before reaching the less steep crater scooped out of the clifftop by the detonation of the shell or bomb. In some cases, the surviving sectionalized Commando ladders were used.

Lieutenant Lapres of Company E and several other Rangers had reached the top where

> a heavy explosion occurred above the rest of 861's team, waiting their turn on the rope. Pfc. Paul L. Medeiros was half buried under debris from the cliff. None of the men knew what caused the explosion, whether a naval shell, or the detonation of a German mine of a peculiar type found later at one or two places along the cliff edge. The enemy had hung naval shells (200mm or larger) over the edge, attached by wire to a pull-type firing device and fitted with a short-delay time fuse. The explosion had no effect on the escalade.

During this vulnerable period when the Rangers were struggling up the cliff, not only was ML 304 helping subdue the enemy positions to the east of the point whose enfilade fire was proving so dangerous but USS *Satterlee* as well. Observing that the Rangers were in difficulty, one naval officer reported that 'I immediately ordered *Satterlee* to close the point and take the cliff tops under fire . . .' She came dashing at high speed to a matter of hundreds of yards from the rocky coast and shells from *Satterlee*'s 5in guns were soon detonating across the battery. These rounds prevented

Climbing the rope proved to be much harder than in training.

the Germans from making an organized effort against the Rangers when they held every advantage. As elsewhere in the V US Corps' area, the Allied navies played a significant role in getting the army ashore and keeping them ashore.

The SWANs, having been unable to get near enough to the cliff, were not entirely redundant and also provided some fire support. One under command of Sergeant Stiverson elevated its ladder to cliff level, with Stiverson himself manning the twin Vickers K guns mounted behind a steel shield. He bravely engaged the defenders; however, swaying in the wind some distance from the clifftop this fire cannot have been accurate but contributed to the psychological effect on the enemy. He naturally attracted the return fire of the German defenders but the swaying target was difficult to hit. Stiverson, however, was forced to order the ladder to be lowered as the volume of fire directed at him grew.

With the Rangers swarming up the cliff Lieutenant Eikner and his signallers at Rudder's command post spoke into the microphone of his PRC 300 radio, sending the message 'PRAISE THE LORD' to Ranger Force C that they were up the cliff. Out to sea Lieutenant Beevor sent the naval code-word 'BINGO' to Commander Denis

Rangers at the clifftop.

aboard HMS *Prince Charles* but due to earlier signals failure, Lieutenant Colonel Schneider was already well on his way to OMAHA Beach.

Clearing the Battery

Of the 225 Rangers who set out to Pointe du Hoc, approximately 190 made it to the beach. Fifteen men became casualties on the beach or during the escalade and another fifteen were made up of Rudder's command post staff, mortarmen, etc. In addition, there were six British Royal Army Ordnance Corps (RAOC) SWAN drivers now helping to handle the supplies and ammunition that had not been ditched, Lieutenant Colonel Trevor and his staff officer, Lieutenant Eades, RNVR and the two paratroopers who had made their way along the beach. The remaining 160 Rangers fanned out across the battery.

Lieutenant Colonel Rudder's plan for the clearance of the Pointe was simple:

> In essence the attack followed a definite plan and order. As first objectives, each platoon ... had a limited part of the enemy defensive system to reach and deal with. Every man knew what this mission was, and where to go. The outcome was an action without clear pattern in detail, but with very clearly defined results.

The principal and 'chief objectives' were the two newly-built casemates, the four open gun-pits and the observation post (OP) bunker sited on the tip of the Pointe. The OP and Gun No. 3 were assigned to Company E, while Company F was to head for Guns 1 and 2 along with the anti-aircraft position on the edge of the cliff at the battery's eastern end. Company D was to have landed on the western face of the Pointe to clear gun-pit 4 and casemates 5 and 6 at the western end of the battery. However, now inserted between Companies E and F they had further to go and cross the line of advance of Company E.

As the Rangers came up the ropes they took cover in the remains of the enemy's cliff-edge trenches or shell-holes but looking out over the battery they 'found themselves in a bewildering wasteland of ground literally torn to pieces by bombs and heavy naval shells. Expected landmarks were gone; craters and mounds of wreckage were everywhere, obscuring remnants of paths and trenches.'

The bombing and shelling had reduced the battery to a moonscape of craters.

The Rangers had over the previous days examined air photographs and detailed maps that showed the latest progress of construction and had memorized landmarks but:

Now, they found themselves in danger of losing their way as soon as they made a few steps from the ragged cliff edge into

128

The forward edge of the command/observation post showing the marks of a direct hit.

the chaos of holes and debris. Obtaining cover was no problem, but maintaining contact within groups as large as a squad would be almost impossible during movement.

As soon as a group of three or four men reached the top of any rope, they set off immediately towards their objective. They did so without waiting for the rest of their section, as the tactics in which they had trained emphasized small bodies of Rangers moving as quickly as possible. This meant that no time was wasted forming up into sections or platoons or even bothering to coordinate with sections coming up neighbouring ropes. Such a plan would only work with specially-selected and trained men with the highest motivation to take the battle to the enemy on their own initiative. Indeed, during 'the climbing phase, so intent were the men on their own work that only in exceptional cases was any Ranger party aware of what other groups were doing.' Sergeant Lomell described his advance towards the western part of the battery from the clifftop:

> We didn't stop. We played it just like a football game, charging hard and low. We went into the shell craters for protection,

129

The forward edge of the command/observation post, as it is today, still showing the marks of the direct hit.

because there were snipers around and machine guns firing at us. We'd wait for a moment and when the fire lifted, we were out of that crater and into the next one.

The Rangers coalesced into about twenty small parties spread across the battery heading for the casemates and gun-pits. Reports were soon coming in to Rudder's command post, now located in a cliff-edge crater beneath the eastern anti-aircraft casemate, that there were no guns in the casemates and all there was at the gun-pits were piles of logs that had clearly been arranged to look like the missing guns. Other groups were soon entering the massively-built troop shelters and rounding up a few shocked infantrymen.

American Ranger weapons.

Other than small-arms fire, very little resistance was being put up by the Germans, with survivors being intent on getting away inland. Counts of enemy prisoners, dead and wounded confirmed that most of the defending infantry had indeed fled the bombardment and/or the assault, but as expected most prisoners were from the III/726 Coastal Infantry Regiment.

The only significant resistance was in the area around the battery observation post on the Pointe and from the western anti-aircraft casemate which, being 200 yards from the bulk of the battery, had not received the full attentions of the shelling and bombing. Consequently, it was full of fight and opened fire with automatic weapons on any Ranger who showed himself in the western half of the battery.

Lieutenant Eikner, now at the clifftop command post, issued the code-word 'TILT' confirming that the battery had been taken. The Ranger signallers continued to fight for communications but only achieved sporadic contact on one of their radios, even from this elevated position. The other set had been soaked, and taking it to pieces, drying out the components and reassembling them had not worked.

Action in the Western Area

With the Rangers having advanced through the battery to its southern perimeter, the problem was sniping by lone enemy riflemen who had been missed in the chaos of the shell-holes and smashed concrete. Private Cruz had been slightly wounded during landing but after having his wounds dressed he was sent up the ramp of rubble and ladders to provide protection to the command post. Here they found the CP under fire from a rifleman in the area of gun-pit number 4. He and Ranger Eberle were sent to stalk him

and in doing so we drew machine-gun fire from the anti-aircraft position to the west. Somebody ordered us to 'go after it'. We started out, sliding from cover of one crater to another, and we came up with Sergeant Spleen, Sergeant Mains, and a group of eight or ten Rangers, in cover just west of No. 6 position. This party was considering an attack on the anti-aircraft position, but they hesitated to open fire in case they drew German artillery shells, which were beginning to hit near the fortified area from somewhere inland.

Eventually the Rangers began to dash or crawl from crater to crater towards the anti-aircraft casemate but now they had to be cautious as they were out of the main battery area and into the minefield. A little way ahead a German helmet rose over the lip of a crater but Private Cruz spotted the stick under it and realized that it was a lure to tempt a Ranger to expose his head and shoulders while taking a shot but another Ranger 'took the bait'. Within a minute, artillery shells and mortar bombs started to fall, forcing the Rangers, mainly of Company D, to scatter in all directions in an effort to spread out.

While scattering, Private Cruz had headed back some way towards No. 6 Gun Position where he found himself alone in a wilderness of craters and smashed concrete. After fifteen minutes the enemy artillery and mortar fire reduced and he began to crawl back towards the CP:

Just as I rolled into a ruined trench near No. 6 position, I saw Sergeant Spleen and two other Rangers disappear around the corner of a connecting trench. Suddenly an intense small-arms fire started up, not only from the anti-aircraft position to the west but from German machine pistols close by.

As he crouched in the bottom of the trench, Cruz could hear men moving and a few Germans passed close by but did not see him. 'Then, only a few yards from my hole, rifles were thrown into the air. I thought they came up from the trench where Spleen's party had gone. I kept quiet and the burst of firing died away quickly, and no one else came in sight.'

After another wait, Private Cruz crawled back towards the CP, which was only 200 yards to the east. Near the wrecked No. 6 case-

The westernmost of the casemates, showing significant battle damage.

mate and gun-pit, he passed a pile of US rifles plus some revolvers and 'Tommy' (Thompson) guns. As there were no bodies of fellow Rangers in the area he believed that this was evidence that Rangers had been forced to surrender.

German troops in the western anti-aircraft position were to continue to be a source of serious difficulty as they were able to fire into the centre of the battery and made the business of moving about the Pointe risky.

Action Around the Bunker

The observation post on the Pointe was one of the objectives assigned to Lieutenant Lapres' platoon of Company E. It had, during the landing and escalade phases, been able to enfilade the beach and the Rangers climbing the cliff from the right.

LCA 861 landed close to the Pointe and Lieutenant Lapres and his Rangers were soon up the cliff using the last of their grapples and a plain rope. They found themselves less than 10 yards to the left of the massive concrete observation bunker. As Sergeant Denbo and Private Roberts started to crawl through the badly-damaged trenches he was seen and came under rifle and machine-gun fire from the observation slit. The Rangers threw four grenades

133

at the narrow slit and three went in, exploding inside, but in the process Sergeant Denbo was wounded by a rifle bullet.

Sergeant Yardley brought up a bazooka and with his first shot hit the edge of the firing slit; the second went through. While the Germans were reeling from the effect of the explosions in their casemate, a group of Rangers 'left Yardley to watch the embrasure and dashed around the OP without drawing enemy fire.' On the other side of the bunker they came across Corporal Aguzzi and several others who had been similarly attempting to subdue the position from the other side. In the chaos of the battle, each was unaware of the presence of the other.

The Rangers may have subdued the fire from the bunker but its massive structure still protected the Germans inside and was impervious to their attempts to damage it and get them out. The demolition charges had been left down on the beach and in the prevailing conditions they were too far away to consider being fetched. The enemy, however, was 'buttoned-up' inside and once the radio antenna had been shot away, they were without communications.

The Beach

Back down on the beach the situation was scarcely less dangerous as the Rangers and British SWAN RAOC drivers unloading the LCAs were still under sustained fire from the enemy position to the east. This fire prevented the Rangers setting up their 60mm and 81mm mortars on the beach and slowed the process of off-loading the craft. The natural inclination was for men to stay in cover as

An enemy position on the headland to the east was the source of most of the fire onto the beach below the Pointe.

long as possible. Lieutenant Colonel Trevor, dressed in British battledress but wearing a US helmet, realized that this was one of those cases when 'occasional acts of gallantry are necessary to give men courage in battle.' To that end, he nonchalantly strode around the beach with an unusual gait and when questioned about this by a Ranger he explained: 'They can't take a bead on me. I take two short steps and three long ones and they always miss me.' A short time later a

Lieutenant Colonel Tom Trevor.

ricochet hit the front of his helmet, driving the metal from the rim into Lieutenant Colonel Trevor's forehead and hurling him into a shell crater. As Rangers ran to pull him out, he stood up and looked across the bay to the left and growled out of the corner of his mouth: 'The dirty bastard.'

Chapter Seven

Ranger Force C at OMAHA Beach

Following Exercise FABIUS in May, the Provisional Ranger Group's plan had been changed. If the cliff assault was successful, Ranger Force C would land behind Lieutenant Colonel Rudder's Ranger Force A but if the assault was unsuccessful or the code-word for success ('TILT') had not been received by 0700 hours Lieutenant Colonel Schneider, with Companies A and B of the 2nd Rangers and his own 5th Ranger Battalion would be slotted into the waves of landing craft heading for OMAHA Beach DOG GREEN Sector. Once ashore, they would infiltrate by platoons to a rendezvous point (RV) at the Ormel Farm and from there head west to Pointe du Hoc, which they were expected to reach by 1300 hours.

Ranger Force C boarded their LCAs half an hour after Rudder's men and having assembled, circling around their mother ships, set off at 0500 hours for the coast of Normandy. The landing craft of the 501st, 504th and 507th flotillas made about 5 knots and had the same difficulties in maintaining their stations in the 3ft waves and of course the Rangers were also soaked and cold.

At 0550 hours, as the flotillas were passing through the bombardment force some 13,000 yards from the coast, the line of ships including USS *Texas* opened fire. The great gouts of orange flame and smoke as the ships unleashed their broadsides plus, of course, the solid wall of sound momentarily stunned the men crammed into the hulls of the LCAs.

At about 8,000 yards out one of Company F's 5th Battalion landing craft with the company commander aboard was swamped and had to be abandoned. The Rangers and crew were, however, picked up by an LCT and later put ashore on OMAHA Beach.

By 0615 hours (H-15) the Rangers were approaching their station 2 miles off Pointe de la Percée and at 0630 started circling ready to go either to Pointe du Hoc or to OMAHA. It was a long wait and as the radio nets burst into life the diminutive craft with far from powerful radios aboard struggled to hear anything intelligible.

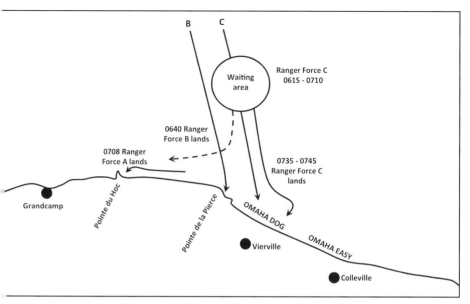

Landing of Ranger Forces B and C.

Landing options for Ranger Force C.

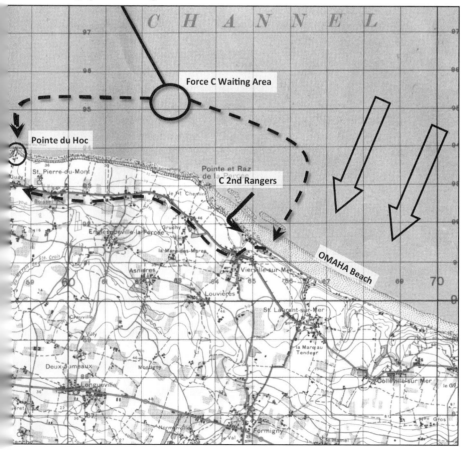

Aboard one of the landing craft from the 507th Assault Flotilla, Lieutenant Raaen was just one of those officers expecting the code-word from Ranger Force A at around H+15:

> By 0700 hours, or H+30, we were frantic. No message of any sort had been received from the 2nd. Over our SCR 300 radio, we had heard a call from a beach master saying, in effect, that 'OMAHA DOG WHITE is clear of enemy. Assault forces meeting no resistance.' Finally we heard a feeble radio message that could have been from the 2nd Rangers. It was almost un-intelligible, but it did contain a word that sounded like 'Charlie'. We weren't sure what it meant, but it clearly did not mean success.

Commander Dennis aboard HMS *Prince Charles* was responsible for dispatching his landing craft to either option but at 0700 hours, with no word from Pointe du Hoc, he passed the order to the flotilla to take Ranger Force C to OMAHA. Shortly afterwards, with her powerful radio and mast-mounted antennas high above sea level, HMS *Prince Charles* picked up the first message from Lieutenant Eikner's 2nd Rangers' signallers but could no longer communicate with Ranger Force C to change the orders. Even though Lieutenant Colonel Schneider had delayed an additional ten minutes beyond his 0700 hours cut-off, by the time the success signal was sent the three flotillas of LCAs, each in double column, had already turned their bows towards OMAHA.

Ranger Force C: First Wave

Companies A and B and half the headquarters of the 2nd Ranger Battalion aboard the 501st Assault Flotilla were fitted into the assault wave scheduled to land on DOG GREEN at 0730 hours (H+60), but because of the extra time spent waiting for the signal from Ranger Force A they were running about ten minutes late. Ahead of them the bluffs were wreathed in smoke and dust from the detonation of shells and burning scrub. On the beach knocked-out tanks and bursting mortar bombs were visible but barely discernible in the surf were the survivors of the 1st Battalion, 116th US Infantry Regiment. The tide was also rapidly rising, covering the German beach obstacles.

Sent to the east by the current, the LCAs were heading to the left part of DOG GREEN and were soon under small-arms, mortar

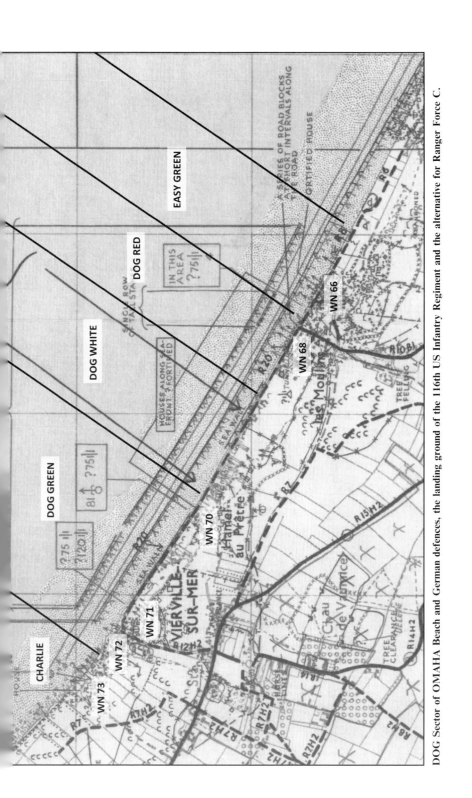

DOG Sector of OMAHA Beach and German defences, the landing ground of the 116th US Infantry Regiment and the alternative for Ranger Force C.

COAST FROM TRANSPORT AREA

With maximum visibility, the coast should be seen from bridge height in the center of the Transport Area (20,000 yards off shore) from GRANDCAMP-LES-BAINS on the right to COUR-SEULLES on the left, with PORT-EN-BESSIN due south. The coast should appear to be practically level, with a maximum height to the right of PORT-EN-BESSIN, tapering slightly to the PORNTE DU HOE on the right and to ARROMANCHES on the left. The 4 1/4 mile stretch of cliff from Exit D1 (VIERVILLE) to POINTE DU HOE should be distinguishable. The Exit valleys D1, D3, E1 and E3 are much less likely to show. On the left of the OMAHA Beach Area, to the left of FOX

GREEN Beach, the ten-mile stretch of cliff broken by valleys should be distinguishable as far as ARROMANCHES. The only man-made objects which may be discernible in the assault area are the spires of VIERVILLE and COLLEVILLE, as well as the houses on the shore at LES MOULINS. PORT-EN-BESSIN and ARROMANCHES should be distinguishable as towns. The chances are against such visibility. At dawn the coast from ARROMANCHES to the gap at PORT-EN-BESSIN should be the most discernible section, being nearest the east.

EAST RED

COLLEVILLE

FOX GREEN

648915 T71

NOT VISIBLE
CHURCH SPIRE

VIERVILLE

PORT-EN-BESSIN

655912 T67

NOT VISIBLE

HAMEL AU PRETRE

tween the beach and the bluff. Most of the houses visible in the assault area are on this flatland in Sector DOG. The houses are at Exit D1, at LES MOULINS (Exit D3), and in between, in two groups at HAMEL AU PRETRE.

SECTOR DOG

DOG
GREEN
970 yards

The valley at Exit D1 marks the right flank of DOG GREEN Beach. The village of VIERVILLE will be visible above the bluff behind the right half of the beach. It has a church spire which should be conspicuous, if not already destroyed. Almost the entire beach is backed by a 6-12 foot seawall which slopes at an angle of 45 degrees. A number of breakwaters (retards) extends from the right portion of the wall. To the left, the wall diminishes in height and terminate 100 yards from the left flank of the beach, where a 4-8 foot wave-cut embankment begins. The left flank is marked by the central large house in the left group at HAMEL AU PRETRE. A paved road runs behind the wall and turns inland at Exit D1.

DOG
GREEN
970 yards

An extract from the OMAHA navigation aid showing DOG Sector.

The view of DOG 1 from a landing craft on D+1.

and artillery fire. While approaching the beach the ramp of Lieutenant Fitzsimmons' LCA carrying his platoon of Company B hit
a mine or shell that tipped one of the now submerged obstacles,
which the engineers who had been landed earlier were unable to
clear from the fire-swept beach. The Rangers were in the water
swimming and dragging their unconscious platoon commander
towards the shore. Seconds later the first of the LCAs grounded
almost directly in front of Wn 70 up on the bluffs. It was an easy
task for the German machine-gunners to send bursts of fire into the
landing craft as their ramps dropped and the Rangers struggled
through the narrow exit one by one. Lieutenant Brice, also of Company B, paused on the ramp of his LCA and, turning to encourage
his men, was hit in the chest by a burst of fire and died instantly.

Those who made it onto the sands, with the same determination
to 'Get off the beach' as shown earlier by Ranger Force B, had to
run the gauntlet of enfilade by fire from the right, coming from
Wn 71, 72 and that part of Wn 73 that Captain Goranson's Company C had yet to secure. The open beach was soon littered with
dead and dying Rangers. It is estimated that only sixty-five men
from the headquarters and Companies A and B of the 2nd Rangers
made it to the dubious cover of the sea wall; that is to say there
were just over 60 per cent casualties. The disaster that had befallen
the 1st Battalion, 116th Infantry and those others who had preceded the Rangers onto DOG GREEN had been played out again.

141

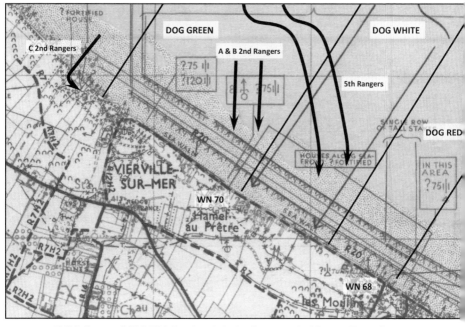

DOG GREEN DOG WHITE

C 2nd Rangers A & B 2nd Rangers

5th Rangers

DOG RED

DOG Sector of OMAHA Beach and the landing ground of Ranger Force C.

The 5th Rangers: Landing

Just five minutes and little more than half a mile behind Companies A and B, Lieutenant Colonel Schneider saw what was happening to the 2nd Rangers on DOG GREEN. As a veteran of the TORCH landings in North Africa, the assault on the Sicilian coast and that on Anzio, he was not going to throw his men into an inferno if he didn't have to. Sergeant Graves, Schneider's radio operator, recalled that the colonel

> asked his flotilla officer to shift the landing of the 5th Rangers about six to eight hundred yards to the east where he could see the beach was quieter. The British crews accomplished this maneuver despite being under increasing fire and despite being less than a thousand yards off shore.

As the crews were manoeuvring towards DOG WHITE, curiosity and the strong urge to peer over the side at what was happening to their front was in danger of getting the better of some Rangers. Sergeant Groves recalled that Schneider ordered all the men in his boat to stand up and to look straight ahead. He said: 'That's where you are going to land. Now sit down and don't for any reason stand up.'

142

The scene as the craft headed for the beach was similar to that facing the 2nd Rangers with shells exploding, machine-gun fire cracking overhead and craft sinking but miraculously none of the 5th Rangers' craft were hit or fell victim to obstacles and mines but it was a close-run thing as Lieutenant Raaen recalled:

Waves lashed at us, throwing the boat to left and right, pitching, tossing, smashing into German obstacles. At one point, we were crashing down on a pole-type obstacle with a Teller mine wired to it. 'Too bad, this is it,' I thought. But another wave grabbed us, throwing us to the left and a few moments later [past] the rest of the obstacles.

Unlike Ranger Force A, the 507th Assault Flotilla was able to deploy properly from its double column into line with the LCAs

The simplest of beach obstacles: a Teller mine on a stake.

25 yards apart as they threaded their way through the obstacles. Together they touched down at 0745 hours on the boundary between DOG WHITE and DOG RED. The 5th Battalion's second wave came in five minutes behind and slightly to the right, which gave the battalion a combined frontage of some 200 yards.

Lieutenant Colonel Schneider had landed his battalion in the gap between Wn 68 and Wn 70, both of which were concentrating at that moment on landings closer to them. While the 5th Rangers were certainly subjected to machine-gun fire, it was nothing like the deadly and intense fire on DOG GREEN. Consequently, the 450 Rangers plus attached signallers crossed the beach at speed and reached the cover of the stone groynes and the wooden palisade sea wall having suffered only five casualties. Arriving at the sea wall was the first time that many Rangers realized that they had not been landed at their intended spot; they had been expecting the concrete sea wall that backed DOG GREEN.

The 5th Rangers found themselves with elements of C Company, 116th Infantry. *American Forces in Action* commented that:

> Both units were in relatively good condition after the landings and had suffered only minor losses, but the men were crowded shoulder to shoulder, sometimes several rows deep, along the shingle at the base of the timber sea wall. Intermingled with

The landing of Ranger Force C.

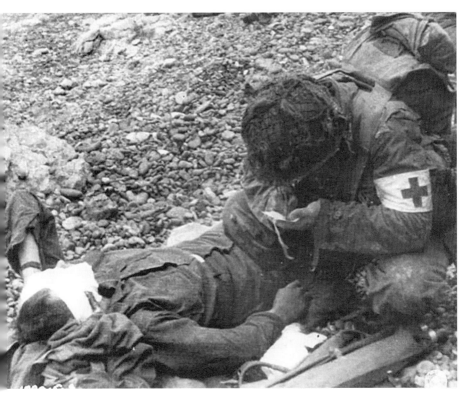

A medic treating a casualty on the beach.

these troops were one or two boat sections from other units of the 116th, and some engineer elements.

These soldiers, mostly in action for the first time, who had endured shelling during their run-in to OMAHA and a sprint across the fire-swept beach to cover, were disorganized and naturally reluctant to leave the shelter of the sea wall. Reorganization was taking place but it took example and the steadfast leadership of Brigadier General Norman Cota, deputy commander of the 29th US Infantry Division, who had landed with his headquarters just ahead of the Rangers at 0730 hours, to get things moving again.

Meanwhile, as seen by Lieutenant Raaen through the clouds of smoke billowing around the bluffs, off to the right men were moving across the flat ground beyond the sea wall. These were elements of the 116th Infantry and survivors of Companies A and B of the 2nd Rangers. They were among the first to leave the main part of the beach but were few in number. It was approaching 0800 hours and they were heading towards Wn 70 on the top of the bluff.

One of the 743rd Tank Battalion's Shermans knocked out on OMAHA Beach with the bluffs in the background.

The 2nd Rangers on the Bluffs

The next wave of Shermans of the 743rd Tank Battalion, who had driven off their LCTs behind the Rangers and had helped them cross the beach, opened fire on the German positions off to the right. Their task, with the failure of the DD tanks earlier, was now to neutralize or destroy surviving German positions, particularly the concrete machine-gun emplacements. At the same time the navy's destroyers, realizing that the Germans had pinned assault troops down on the beach, had come in-shore to dangerously shallow water to observe and take on targets with direct fire. At the same time, 13,000 yards out to sea the ships of the bombardment force, including USS *Texas*, engaged the bluffs above the Rangers. Neutralizing the German defenders was absolutely key to breaking the stalemate on the beach and later in the day V US Corps' commander General Gerow said: 'Thank God for the United States Navy.'

The 2nd Rangers' Company A was now commanded by Sergeant John White, all the officers having become casualties on the beach, but Captain Arnold had survived the sprint to cover and lead the eighteen survivors of Company B. Together with a handful of

146

The Vierville draw (DOG 1) under naval gunfire.

The routes taken by Ranger Force C up the bluffs and inland.

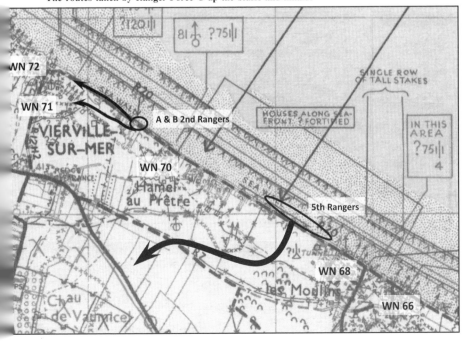

D Company, 116th Infantry, Company B's first move from cover below Wn 70 was to make their way west under the concrete sea wall towards the Vierville draw (DOG 1), with the intent of infiltrating through the German defences and reach Pointe du Hoc. As they approached Wn 72 at the mouth of the draw, they were abruptly halted by heavy machine-gun fire, suffering casualties, and they were forced to withdraw.

The Rangers of Company A followed Company B but on a different route, moving through the ruined beach villas and up the bluffs towards Wn 71. This required them to cut the barbed wire that was still intact despite the preliminary bombardment. Their first attempt by Private Lambert to get up out of cover, cross the beach road and place a Bangalore torpedo under the wire failed when, presumably after its soaking during the run-in and landing, the fuse would not ignite. Lieutenant Schwartz was more successful and Company A and surviving parts of D Company, 116th Infantry dashed through the gap into the cover of the ruins.

With machine-gunners from Company D providing covering fire, the Rangers, enraged by their casualties on the beach, reached the crest and, 'shouting obscenities at any Germans they spotted', charged headlong out of the smoke at the German position as the wire here had been well shredded by the bombardment. The enemy fled, unnerved by this sudden and violent eruption. Sergeant Courtney and Private Breher found trenches flanked by several machine-gun positions abandoned by the enemy. They were followed by six other Rangers from Company A who set about working their way

Widerstandsnest **71 and 72.**

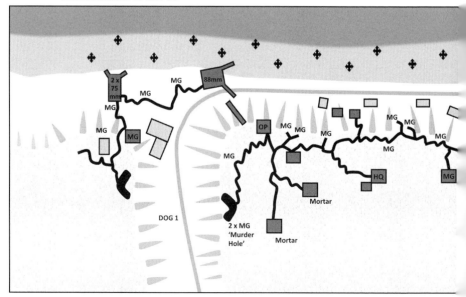

A pre-war postcard looking west to the Vierville draw and Wn 71, 72 and 73 past the villas through which Company A advanced.

through the trench system. The Germans had, however, only withdrawn a short distance and the Rangers were soon pinned down by fire from the mouths of two concrete casemates. This required the rest of Company A, some twenty Rangers, to fire and manoeuvre into a position from which they could assault the emplacements. This they did, killing six Germans in the process and taking another six prisoners at a cost of three Ranger casualties.

Despite this success, the Rangers had come up against the mutually-supporting German positions that guarded DOG 1, the Vierville draw. Here they were halted.

The 5th Rangers on the Bluffs

Meanwhile, the 5th Rangers had been reorganizing themselves and reporting to Lieutenant Colonel Schneider prior to beginning their infiltration to the Ranger RV on the code-word 'TALLY HO'. Mortars were set up, a pair of engineers set up a Browning machine gun and Bangalore torpedoes were prepared to breach the enemy barbed wire. *American Forces in Action* describes the ground beyond the palisade sea wall, beach road and the barbed wire:

The sector was relatively favorable for an advance across the beach flat and up the bluff. The nearest enemy strongpoints

149

were several hundred yards off to either flank, and no concentrated fire was hitting the area congested with assault troops. In front of them, heavy smoke from grass fires on the bluff was drifting eastward along the face of the slope. From the sea wall to the foot of the rise was only 150 yards, but the flat ground, with patches of marsh near the hill, was nearly devoid of cover.

The first part of the 5th Rangers to move was Lieutenant Parker's Company A as recorded in the US War Department notes:

Lieutenant Ace Parker, having the farthest to go, immediately moved back to A Company and gave Hathaway, his Bangalore torpedo man, orders to blow a hole in the barbed wire that barred passage to the high ground beyond the beach. After the Bangalore had done its work, Parker, followed by A Company, dashed through the gap, across the flat, and began to climb the bluffs to his front. The smoke from the brush fire had two benefits, it obscured A Company's advance from the Germans dug in at the crest and it burned away the brush, exposing many of the mines emplaced on the flat area in front of the bluffs and on the slopes of the bluff itself. The smoke also served to disorganize the movement. Many Rangers had to put on their gas masks to get through the smoke and some were momentarily lost. Contact between platoons and sections was rarely maintained. Lieutenant Suchier, A Company, went into the smoke leading his platoon and came out with only two men.

Brigadier General Cota had, meanwhile, been making his way east under cover of the palisade sea wall. Stories of the general's actions in staving off defeat at this time abound but Captain Raaen, who was preparing to lead his men through a freshly-blown gap, had his own story:

As I got ready to move out, I saw, or had pointed out to me, a man casually wandering down the beach toward us. It was clear that he was someone with authority, for he was shouting orders and encouragement to the troops huddled against the seawall or burrowing into the edge of the embankment. By the time he got to our vicinity, I realized he was quite high-ranking, a colonel or general. I jumped up, ran over to him, saluted, and reported, 'Captain Raaen, 5th Ranger Infantry Battalion, Sir!' 'Raaen, Raaen, yes, you must be Jack Raaen's son. I'm General Cota. What's the situation here?' 'Sir, the 5th Rangers have landed intact here and to the east about 200 yards. The battalion commander has ordered us to proceed by platoon infiltration to our rendezvous points.' He asked where Lieutenant Colonel Schneider was located. I pointed out the bay where Schneider was sitting against the seawall, still talking with one or two of the company commanders. I offered to take him to Schneider, but he said, 'No. You stay here with your men.' He started toward Schneider, then stopped and turned to the troops in my vicinity and said, 'You men are Rangers. I know you won't let me down.' And with that, he was off ... shouting 'You have to get off the beach or you're gonna die.'

Brigadier General Norman Cota.

Others record that Cota said: 'Gentlemen, we are being killed on the beaches. Let us go inland and be killed.' This sounds far more like a brigadier general!

On reaching Schneider's headquarters and despite being under fire, after an exchange of salutes Brigadier General Cota gave the Rangers' commanding officer orders, changing their mission to one of helping Colonel Canham's 116th Infantry establish a beachhead. Sergeant Graves recalled what was said: 'Colonel, you are going to have to lead the way. We are bogged down. We've got to get these men off this God-damned beach.'

Lieutenant Jack Shae, Cota's aide-de-camp, recalled more detail:

Cota ordered Schneider to blow the wire and lead the 5th Rangers against the enemy fortifications at Pointe et Raz de la Percée. It was these forts, lying between the Vierville exit [DOG 1] and the Pointe et Raz that were shelling the assault boats as they landed on the OMAHA beaches.

The change of mission, even if Ranger Force C could infiltrate to their rendezvous, of course meant that Rudder's expected relief at 1300 hours would at best be badly delayed. In the confusion on the beach, not all of Schneider's subordinate commanders received the revised orders.

151

A heavily-laden engineer detachment carrying Bangalore torpedoes.

As the 5th Rangers' Bangalores blew the wire in front of Company D at 0810 hours Brigadier General Cota turned to the nearest men and instructed them with the now famous words 'Rangers, lead the way.' Heading up the bluffs between two *Widerstandsnest*, the Rangers greatly benefited from naval gunfire on Wn 70 and elements of the 116th Infantry attacking Wn 68. In both cases the enemy had their own problems which distracted them from providing interlocking and overlapping arcs of fire across the bluff's open slope.

The Rangers moved off by platoons, rushing across the road through the six gaps they had blown in the barbed wire and over flat ground to the base of the bluffs which they proceeded to climb in almost single file preceded by scouts. The columns threaded their way around real and dummy minefields as well as around patches of burning scrub and banks of smoke. In the fifteen minutes it took

Placing several sections of Bangalore under a wire obstacle.

The resulting explosion shredded barbed wire and detonated mines.

The bluffs shown on a pre-war postcard, taken overlooking the area where the 5th Rangers climbed them.

the leading elements of the 5th Battalion to reach the crest there was some mortar and machine-gun fire when the smoke swirled to reveal the Rangers but no enemy were encountered during the climb. Remarkably, it is estimated that the battalion suffered only eight casualties in climbing the bluffs. All that, however, changed as the leading Rangers reached the crest.

As the 2nd Rangers had been, the men of the 5th Battalion were quickly into scantily-manned German trenches between Wn 68 and Wn 70. The Germans that stood were dealt with but most hurried away. Lieutenant Dawson of Company D came up against a concrete machine-gun position that was firing on the beach below. Private Reed fired a rifle grenade – a direct hit into the enemy bunker – but it failed to go off. None the less Lieutenant Dawson, taking the opportunity provided by the confusion among the Germans of a grenade arriving in their midst, charged the position, spraying the enemy liberally with submachine-gun fire.

Shortly after the 2nd Rangers reached the crest near Wn 71, the 5th Rangers were also at the top of the bluffs. The time was 0830 hours and General Bradley aboard his command ship could only glimpse the chaos on the beach and was being fed a stream of bad news from subordinate commanders. He signalled General Dempsey saying that he was going to abandon OMAHA and put

154

the remains of the 29th Division ashore behind the 4th Division on UTAH and would like to put the 1st Division ashore on GOLD Beach. At the same time the 352nd Division's commander, *General-leutnant* Kraiss, was signalling LXXXIV Corps that he had defeated the 'English landing at Vierville'. At this stage neither general was aware that Ranger Force C, along with elements of Colonel Canham's 116th Infantry, had forced their way up the bluffs and were heading inland with others following. Bradley would issue orders for the abandonment of OMAHA at around 0900 hours but cancelled them shortly afterwards once he knew that his troops were fighting above the bluffs.

Brigadier General Cota being decorated with the Distinguished Service Cross (DSC) by General Omar Bradley for his action on the beach on D-Day.

The Advance Inland

In the advance up the bluffs the 5th Battalion had again become unbalanced with platoons criss-crossing as they felt their way upwards through the smoke. Consequently, Schneider halted the companies on the crest-line to reorganize before moving on inland at around 0900 hours.

Initially the main opposition to the Rangers' advance led by Lieutenant Pepper and his platoon of Company B was from widespread small-arms fire, which took a steady toll of Rangers as they fought their way inland, hedgerow by hedgerow, towards Vierville. Soon, however, shells and mortar bombs were added to the small-arms fire, with Lieutenant Colonel Schneider's headquarters being caught in the open as they moved forward behind the companies.

Captain Raaen recalled: 'With scouts out and flank protection, Pepper moved his platoon generally west towards Vierville. However, after a short distance, naval gunfire began landing directly in their path. Lieutenant Pepper wisely turned inland, more towards the south and reached the blacktop coastal highway [D514] about 0930.'

The Germans had, however, spotted Pepper and his men and engaged with rifles and machine guns before they could cross the road. Schneider was forward with Company B and with an enemy positions having been located in the south-west corner of the field ahead of them Lieutenant Pepper was ordered to 'take it out'. As he 'was crossing into the wheat field with the leading section, they saw about twenty Germans leaving the area where the machine gun had been located. Thinking the machine gun position had been abandoned, they started across the field only to be fired on.'

To make matters worse the battalion strung out back to the bluffs and C Company, 116th Infantry who were following along with various survivors of other companies, came under sustained artillery fire. Consequently, even though Lieutenant Pepper's men knocked out a machine gun, they were brought to a halt between 0930 and 1030 hours on the line of the D514. The Rangers had encountered a German position, the bunkers and barbed wire of which had first been marked on the 20 May 'Stop Press' edition of the Defences Overprint map. Attempts to turn the flanks failed and soon Lieutenant Colonel Schneider had four companies strung out along several hundred yards of road.

The Rangers were no longer facing the 'elderly gentlemen' of the coastal troops who held the *Widerstandsnest* overlooking OMAHA

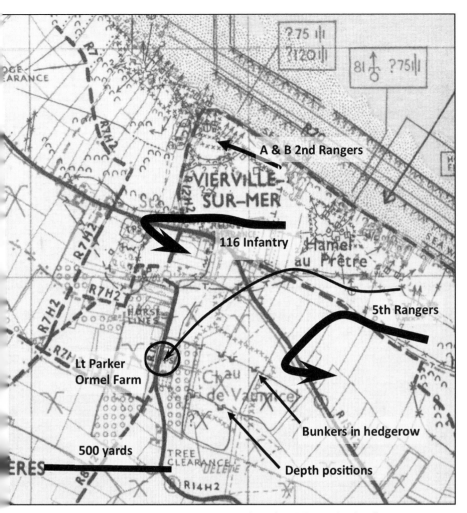

A & B 2nd Rangers

VIERVILLE-SUR-MER

116 Infantry

5th Rangers

Lt Parker Ormel Farm

Bunkers in hedgerow

500 yards

Depth positions

Close-up of the Defences Overprint map east of the Ormel Farm, showing German bunkers in the hedgerows and the surrounding barbed wire. German positions in hedgerows were difficult for air photo interpreters to spot so those shown are probably only a few of those that would have been there.

but had come up against the field-grade infantry of the German 352nd Division dug in among the thick Normandy hedgerows in a well-coordinated defensive system. This second line had been created by leaving in place the 726 *Infanterie-Regiment* when, based on Hitler's intuition, the 352nd had been brought forward to the OMAHA sector of the coast during the early spring. According to the divisional chief of staff *Oberstleutnant* Ziegelmann, the division's training had been greatly disrupted by having to work on the

157

beach obstacles, particularly after the April storm that had washed many of them away, and the infantry were consequently not very well trained. Even so, they represented an altogether higher-quality opposition.

Lieutenant Ace Parker

It will be recalled that Lieutenant Parker, with Lieutenant Zele-pesky's platoon, had been first away leading the 5th Battalion's Company A up the bluffs. He was one of the officers who had not been informed of the change of plan and that they were to assist the 116th Infantry in forming a bridgehead. Instead he stuck to his original orders and infiltrated the 600 yards inland to the D514 coast road via the outskirts of Vierville. The commander of Company A's second platoon that was following was hit and wounded and the delay caused by applying first aid allowed a runner to catch up with them and inform them of the change of plan. Lieutenant Ace Parker and his twenty-three men, plus some Company E men, were now well ahead and could not be brought back as they headed for the Ranger RV at the Ormel Farm.

Lieutenant Ace Parker.

356. **Vierville-sur-Mer** (Calvados) — Ferme de l'Ormel · Sortie des Percherons

The typical Norman Ormel Farm as shown on a pre-war postcard.

Crossing a field, the Rangers came under fire from the hedgerow opposite; Lieutenant Parker had run into the companies of the II/916 *Infanterie-Regiment* who had been deployed within a mile of the beach. This was almost certainly the same enemy position that the rest of the battalion had hit further to the east. Two men were hit and wounded and the platoon was driven into a ditch where they were pinned down for several hours before they managed to infiltrate past the enemy position. Out on their own, having made the two casualties as comfortable as possible before leaving them behind, Parker and his men moved on.

Lieutenant Parker reached the Ormel Farm around midday and was eventually joined by a platoon of B Company, 116th Infantry led by Lieutenant Taylor. However, with no evidence of the rest of the 5th Rangers, Parker moved on via minor roads to the next rendezvous, a crossroads 1,000 yards west. Encountering slight opposition in farm buildings and rounding up prisoners en route to the RV, again there was no sign of the rest of the battalion. Parker and Zelepesky concluded that they must have moved on to Pointe du Hoc and set off along the narrow high-hedged lane to the small village of Englesqueville-la-Percée. This inland route for the infiltration had been originally selected during planning to avoid likely enemy troop movements on the coastal road (D514).

159

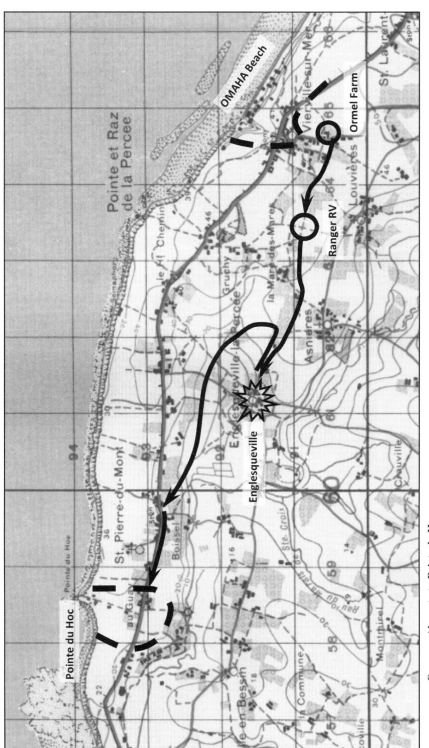

Company A's route to Pointe du Hoc.

The Englesqueville Ferme shown on a pre-war postcard.

After almost 2 miles, during which the Rangers rounded up more prisoners in a minor engagement, they were approaching Englesqueville and here their luck ran out. A few vague markings on the Defences Overprint map proved to be a significant German position, namely 9 *Kompanie Grenadier-Regiment* III/726, and what is more they had spotted the Rangers! A fire-fight then developed and the Germans were soon heard beyond the hedges manoeuvring through the orchards to left and right. In imminent danger of being enveloped, Lieutenant Parker then ordered the abandonment of the prisoners and a hasty retreat down the road up which they had just come.

Having escaped, the twenty-three Rangers then abandoned the road and struck across country giving Englesqueville a wide berth and infiltrating along hedgerows to St Pierre-du-Mont. Rather than the dangerous course of approaching a friendly force stealthily and risking fratricide, Parker marched his men down the coast road for the last mile before encountering the 2nd Rangers' outposts in the village of Au Guay at 2100 hours. Lieutenant Colonel Rudder was informed and the inevitable question was 'Where are the rest of the 5th Rangers?' None the less, a platoon was a small but welcome reinforcement for the defence of Pointe du Hoc.

161

The Afternoon

Having been halted on the D514 since mid-morning while waiting for artillery support, Captain Raaen noticed that the 5th Rangers' weapons produced visible smoke when fired but those of the Germans, well concealed in bunkers hollowed out of the banked hedgerows, couldn't be seen. Ultimately being unable to break through the German positions and head south, Lieutenant Colonel Schneider then sent Company B 1,000 yards west to Vierville at 1430 hours. With heavy naval gunfire support this village had been captured around midday by Colonel Canham's 116th Infantry against slight opposition. As Company B, 5th Rangers and elements of C Company, 116th attempted to advance west along the coast road from Vierville, within 500 yards they came up against a strong infantry position similar to those that had earlier brought the Rangers to a halt. These two companies battled for over an hour but they could not get through the defences of the II/726 *Infanterie-Regiment*.

During the course of the afternoon a combination of naval gunfire and, with the German logistic organization having broken down under Air Force interdiction, a lack of ammunition, defences generally began to collapse, noticeably so in DOG 1. Relieved in place by the 116th Infantry and engineers during late afternoon Schneider was able to bring the rest of his battalion across to Vierville from where he hoped to be able to begin his advance to Pointe du Hoc.

The Vierville draw, a photo taken by a PRU (Photographic Reconnaissance Unit) Spitfire in 1943 before the fortification of the area had been completed.

With the 116th Infantry having suffered heavy losses and now disordered, Colonel Canham would not countenance the departure of the Rangers as he could not fill the gap left in his line by such a move. Schneider appealed but Canham's decision was supported up the chain of command to General Gerow at V US Corps HQ. The logic was that they could afford to lose the three companies of Rangers at Pointe du Hoc but they could not afford to lose the slim OMAHA bridgehead to German counter-attack, which they were sure would be coming.

The situation at the western end of OMAHA Beach at the end of D-Day.

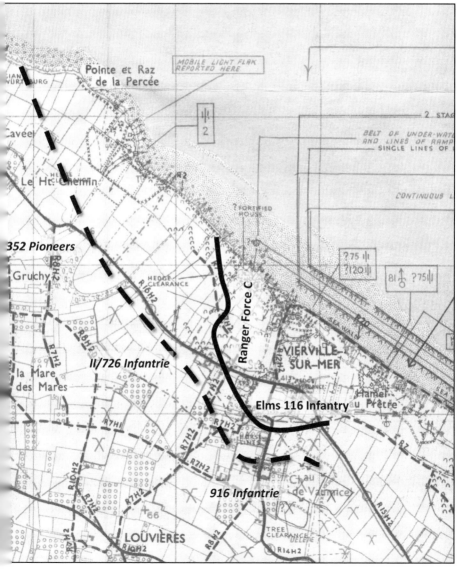

Chapter Eight

Finding the Guns and Holding the Pointe

The moonscape of smashed concrete, shell and bomb craters that was Pointe du Hoc had seen the Rangers fanning out from the cliff, taking on those Germans disposed to fight and taking prisoner enemy soldiers who had had the will to fight knocked out of them by the bombardment. The enemy's guns that they had scaled the cliffs to take were, however, not in either the pits or in the two ostensibly completed casemates. Capturing the Pointe had not delivered the Ranger mission of destroying the six 155mm artillery pieces that could well have been at Pointe du Hoc. It will be recalled that they had been removed sometime after the first issue of the Defences Overprint map in February 1944 and Rommel's much-photographed visit to the site or indeed the first major bombing.

The plan had always been that once the battery area was secured, the Rangers from the three assault companies would advance inland a short distance to secure the area prior to the arrival of troops from OMAHA:

> Most of the force was to push out immediately to the south, reach the coastal highway which was a main communications lateral for German defences of the Grandcamp-Vierville coast, and hold a position controlling that road to the west until the arrival of the 116th Infantry from Vierville. If the assault at OMAHA went according to schedule, the 116th would be at Pointe du Hoe [*sic*] before noon.*

With, however, the Pointe under small-arms and 20mm fire from the flanks and no sign of Ranger Force C out to sea, some Rangers of Company F were retained for the defence of the battery area.

Officers and NCOs of Companies D and E started to gather together their scattered men at the designated rendezvous close to the battery's access road. Advancing south, they came under artillery fire and took cover in a convenient communication trench parallel to the road. As they continued along the trench towards the coast road they again came under artillery fire, probably a mix of

* *American Forces in Action.*

friendly and enemy shells, plus shots from enemy riflemen in the ruins of a farm building. They had, however, gone by the time the Rangers had manoeuvred and broken into the buildings to flush them out. The convenient trench ended and the Rangers were out into more open country. The US historian describes the next stage of the battle:

Beyond the trench a pair of concrete pillars flanked the exit road, with a crude roadblock between the pillars. Three Germans came straight down the road toward the Pointe,

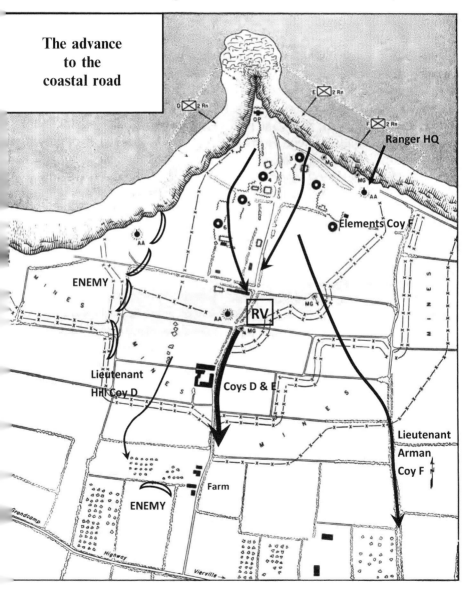

The advance to the coastal road

spotted the Rangers, and ducked behind the block. BAR fire failed to flush them out, but after one round (a dud) from a bazooka the Germans fled. The Rangers resumed their advance down the exit road. Some machine-gun fire had been coming from the next farm; Lieutenant Lapres reached it with his four men to find the enemy had left. For a few minutes Lapres was isolated there, as machine-gun fire from the flanks pinned down the main Ranger party. Some friendly support fire, which the Rangers could not trace, apparently silenced the machine guns.

Meanwhile, on the other flank Company F was holding off probes from the east of the battery along the clifftop. Having become separated, Lieutenant Arman, Sergeant Petty and a handful of men from Company F were making their way, as planned, south from shell-hole to shell-hole across the fields towards the farming hamlet of Au Guay without meeting opposition. This route led them through what was marked on their maps as a minefield. The bombardment had, however, probably sympathetically detonated the mines. In addition, the barbed wire and anti-glider poles had been badly knocked about.

Lieutenant Arman reached the coast road via a track where Petty ventured left across fields to scout towards a château building but found no sign of the enemy marked on their maps and headed back to join Arman. Moving west along the road they approached Au Guay, where a machine gun opened fire on them from cover 100 yards ahead. The Rangers dived into cover without suffering casualties and they

> began to work around the south edge of the hamlet to reach the enemy gun. Sergeant Petty, with two men, was startled by the sudden appearance of two Germans apparently rising out of the ground, not 10 feet away. Petty dropped flat and fired his BAR as he fell. The burst missed, but the Germans were already shouting 'Kamerad'. They had come out of a deep shelter hole which Petty's men had not spotted.

Au Guay was cleared but the machine gun had gone by the time they reached the west side of the hamlet. At some stage in this journey Lieutenant Arman's detachment collected two MG 34s and one MG 42 along with ammunition to add to their fire-power.

Air photo of the coastal road area.

Meanwhile, on the western flank Lieutenant Hill's party of four men was approaching the coast road. He recalled:

We could hear machine-gun fire from near the exit road, and headed in that direction. As we crossed a field we came under automatic fire from the west of Pointe du Hoc and forced us to crawl. The gun we were stalking had not spotted us and was focused on the exit road. At a distance of about 25 feet from the gun Anderson and I were in the cover of a low bank and we could see it ahead across the road. I am told that when I stood up to get a better look at the position I shouted, 'You ****, you couldn't hit a bull in the ass with a bass fiddle!'

This not unnaturally had the enemy swinging the machine gun around to fire at the officer. As he dropped back into cover, Private Anderson tossed Lieutenant Hill one of his grenades which he threw, getting it close enough to stop the machine gun firing.

By 0815 hours approximately fifty Rangers had reached the coastal road. They would, even with both battalions, have found it difficult to 'block' the coast road against armour or large bodies of enemy troops heading east to assemble and mount a counter-attack

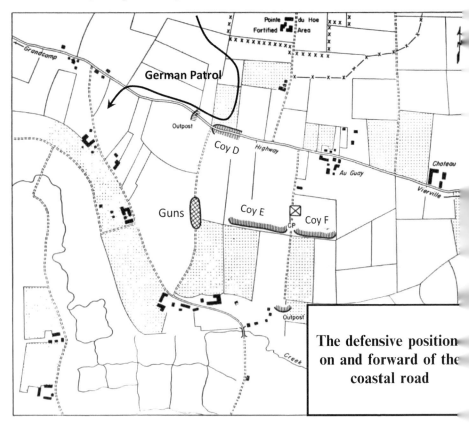

The defensive position on and forward of the coastal road

against the Vierville area. In accordance with their mission they would be able to report on movement on the Grandcamp road but could also help disrupt smaller enemy movement east to OMAHA. The main positions were, in fact, taken up facing south and west beyond the coastal road using foxholes and the odd command dugout that the Germans had built prior to the invasion. It is speculated that these were alternative positions for the infantry defenders of Pointe du Hoc in the event of an enemy advance from inland in order that they could mount a proper defence of the area. The coast road to the west was covered by Company D, while Sergeant Petty was deployed behind a wall in a field further to the south as an outpost. Overlooking the valley, he had a view of what at the time was peaceful countryside.

Finding the Guns

At about 0900 hours, once the defensive line had been established and arcs of fire coordinated, clearance patrols were dispatched to find out what was forward of the thinly-held position. Sergeant Lomell and Staff Sergeant Kuhn from Company D went down a farm track that ran south one field to the west of the defensive line:

> I headed about 250 yards down a double hedge-rowed track to some orchards when I saw tyre marks in the dirt. Following them we almost walked into the trail of a camouflaged gun in one of the hedgerows. Even though they were big guns they were so well covered by trees and camouflage we hadn't noticed them earlier.

Looking around they saw five of the missing 155mm guns deployed to fire towards UTAH Beach but it was the opinion of those who subsequently inspected the position that they could easily have been traversed to engage OMAHA Beach as well. What is more, fused shells were stacked by the guns along with charge bags ready for immediate action but the battery had clearly not yet opened fire. Two and a half hours after H-hour in the US sector it is surprising that a major asset easily in range of DOG GREEN at 6,000 yards was not used during a crucial period. One can only speculate about the reason: a loss of communication, or confusion in the complicated chain of command of coastal batteries? The possible causes of the lack of action by Army Coastal Artillery Battery 2/1260 are endless.

One of the Pointe du Hoc guns concealed in a hedgerow.

Some accounts say that after the battle the sixth gun was found further down the orchard with a damaged carriage, possibly as a result of bombing, and was awaiting removal to workshops.

There were no Germans around the guns but eventually what was estimated to be 100 gunners were spotted gathered together being briefed at the bottom of the field. An opportunity had presented itself to Sergeant Lomell to destroy the guns:

> I said, 'Jack, you cover me and I'm going in there to destroy them.' So, all I had was two thermite grenades – his and mine. I went in and put the thermite grenades in the traversing mechanism, and knocked out two of them because that melted their gears in a moment. And then I broke their sights, and we ran back to the road, which was a hundred or so yards back, and got all the thermites from the remainder of my guys manning the roadblock.

As a part of their assault munitions each company carried ten thermite grenades that were distributed among the Rangers and several more were collected by Lomell and Kuhn. While back at the hedgerow position Sergeant Lunning was dispatched to find Lieutenant Colonel Rudder and tell him that the guns had been found and that 'Company D was dealing with them.' Lomell continued that he

> rushed back and put the grenades in the traversing mechanisms, elevation mechanisms, and banged the sights . . . There is no noise to a thermite, so no one saw us, and Jack said, 'Hurry up and get out of there Len,' and I came up over the hedgerow with him and suddenly the whole place blew up.

This explosion of ammunition was almost certainly the handiwork of Sergeant Rupinski who on a similar clearance patrol had also located and disabled a number of guns by putting thermite grenades in their breaches rather than the elevating mechanism. Twenty minutes after Sergeant Lunning a second Ranger, this time from Company E, arrived at Rudder's command post with the news that Rupinski had destroyed the guns! Either way the 155s had been destroyed but the question of allocating credit and recognition remained. Eventually Rudder awarded the Distinguished Service Cross, America's second-highest honour, for destroying the guns to Sergeant Lomell. He was the first to report and Rudder was not able to hear Rupinski's version of events as he was taken prisoner on D+1. He received the Bronze Star but not his share of the credit.

German gunners loading charge bags into the breach of a heavy gun.

Sergeant Lomell (left) posing with one of the guns after the battle.

The Command Post

With the main part of the battery reported as clear and the Rangers starting to move down to the coast road, Rudder established his clifftop command post at 0745 hours. It was sheltered in a large bomb or shell crater just beneath the damaged eastern anti-aircraft casemate. Getting to and from it was to run a gauntlet of fire from the German position on the cliffs 500 yards to the east. This position had been one of Company F's objectives but they could not reach it, so well was the ground covered by fire. Observing the problem this position was causing, HMS *Talybont* eventually dealt with it by gunfire that blew down a chunk of cliff complete with Germans.

Meanwhile to the west, with shellfire and the enemy active in that area particularly around the anti-aircraft casemate at that end of the battery, moving about anywhere on Pointe du Hoc was increasingly dangerous. Judicious dashes from shell-hole to shell-hole reduced the risk but anyone found unduly 'skulking' by the British Commando liaison officer Lieutenant Colonel Tom Trevor, now with his head swathed in bandages, was accused of 'shirking his duty'.

The Ranger CP during D+1.

Rudder's CP was crowded, so Lieutenant Harwood's twelve-man Naval Shore Fire Control Party (NSFCP) was moved to a nearby bunker where they could work effectively.

To find more room and cover for the HQ, Tom Trevor investigated the lower story of the eastern anti-aircraft casemate, which once cleaned out became a safe place for the Rangers' medical aid post to be established for the duration of the battle. It too, however, also soon became crowded as casualties mounted.

Once on the clifftop, radio communication, though still 'difficult', improved but there was no contact with Ranger Force C and those they could talk to would not, without the correct authentication and codes, pass Lieutenant Eikner any information as to the situation. It was also speculated that accurate artillery fire on the CP was the result of the Germans triangulating their radio signals. This was of course a disincentive to use radio but Morse code by Aldis lamp via the attached NSFCP to USS *Satterlee* had been established at 0728 hours. From that point on and throughout the following two days, fire support could be called on quickly and efficiently from this and other Allied destroyers, namely *Thompson*,

The eastern anti-aircraft position and access to its lower level.

Harding and *Talybont*. This fire was invaluable in helping to keep in check German counter-attacks that were beginning to develop.

None the less, the isolated Rangers needed to impress on their superiors how tenuous was their hold on Pointe du Hoc. Eventually, Rudder ordered Lieutenant Eikner to send the message by radio, messenger pigeon and lamp. Summarized to be as short as possible, the message read: 'Located Pointe du Hoc – mission accomplished – need ammunition and reinforcements – many casualties.' The 116th Infantry responded saying that they could not decode the message and some hours later *Satterlee* signalled back, passing on an even briefer reply 'No reinforcements available.' During this period USS *Barton* attempted to get a boat to the beach to evacuate the wounded but enemy machine-gun fire drove it back. The Rangers were well and truly on their own.

The German garrison, many of whom had been involved in the construction of the battery, knew their way around and were available to guide the reinforcements from Grandcamp who began to infiltrate back into it, particularly from the west. The first reinforcement to the Pointe was almost certainly from 12 *Kompanie* III/726 *Grenadier-Regiment*. The 352nd Division's war diary states that in the mid-morning they also ordered forty men of *Grenadier-Regiment* 914 to march from Osmanville, which was 6 miles away and they, therefore, would not be available until after midday. Recapture of the battery area and the elimination of the CP was the aim of the German attack; destroy that and the Rangers further inland, cut off from support and resupply, could be dealt with at leisure! There was only a small group of men to defend Rudder's CP and drive back the infiltrators. Among the Rangers of headquarters and Company F there were the two paratroopers and at least two of the British RAOC DUKW/SWAN drivers, plus the walking wounded. With so few men, even with the help of the navy, the enemy was only just kept away.

The RAOC soldiers, Corporal Good and Private Blackmore, had scaled the cliffs using the rope ladders and joined the Rangers in the fight as riflemen. When ammunition was running low, they went back down the cliffs and recovered machine guns from the DUKWs, which were then still under fire. They returned back up

Lieutenant Colonel Rudder at the CP still wearing his D-Day gas-mask case on his chest. Note the Aldis signal lamp to the left.

The easiest route up the cliff: a scramble up the ramps of rubble, a short climb and into the shell/bomb crater below the eastern anti-aircraft position.

the cliff and brought the machine guns into action. In doing this Private Blackmore was wounded in the foot. After receiving first aid, he continued to defend the CP and later rescued a badly-wounded Ranger while under machine-gun and mortar fire. He subsequently volunteered to distribute ammunition to the defenders,

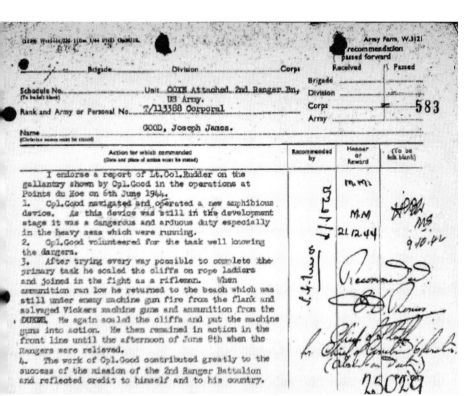

Corporal Good's citation for his Military Medal. Private Blackmore received the same award.

The Military Medal.

salvage ammunition from the beach and repair weapons. He was finally evacuated on 7 June.

During the late morning Rudder received a flesh wound to his leg when he was shot making his way to join the NSFCP. Wound cleaned and bandaged, he remained with the naval party directing the ship's gunfire. He was still there when a non-explosive marker round from one of the cruisers smashed against the bunker. This drop shot unfortunately killed Lieutenant Harwood, USN and further injured Rudder who once again chose to remain on duty and in command.

The CP was able to speak to the companies deployed south of the coastal road by telephone but the surface-laid cable was repeatedly cut by shellfire and the German infiltrators necessitating signallers going out to repair it, with all the risks that entailed. Even this was not possible for much of the afternoon while German troops were in the south of the battery area.

The 352nd Infantry Division's war diary records a conversation between the chief of staff and LXXXIV Corps HQ at St Lo at 1225 hours (1325 Allied time): 'The occupation troops at St P [St Pierre-du-Mont], Pointe du Hoc are encircled by two companies. A counter-attack with part of III/726 *Grenadier-Regiment* has been launched.'

The first organized counter-attack on the CP did not come bowling in from the hedgerows to the west but was mounted from within the battery by German infantry who had been infiltrating it for some time. This attack was beaten off relatively easily but a second emanating from the area of the western anti-aircraft position, which fired in support of the attacking troops, got a lot closer before the Rangers, using up valuable small-arms and mortar ammunition, managed to stop it. Activity subsided during the early evening with the Rangers being subjected to regular bursts of enemy fire.

At about 2100 hours, as already recorded, the Rangers received the reinforcement of Lieutenant Parker and his twenty-two men who were promptly given a sector of hedgerow to defend south of

Ranger HQ signallers.

the coastal road. This brought the strength there up to eighty-plus men. Lieutenant Colonel Rudder, who had been expecting that this first contact from OMAHA heralded imminent relief, spoke to Parker by telephone demanding 'Where the hell is the rest of the 5th Battalion?'

Counter-Attacks

Still with the expectation that the 5th Rangers would be arriving shortly, Rudder decided to leave the forward position in place rather than draw them in to thicken up the CP defence line. The five lieutenants had seen evidence of the enemy since the detonation of the artillery ammunition but had been little bothered by them. The official report states:

> The main action of the day was vigorous and continued patrolling, undertaken by combat patrols of six or seven men who went out on the flanks of the highway position, and particularly to the south into the small valley. The patrols found no organized enemy positions and encountered no strong forces. A number of Germans who had evidently been by-passed near the Pointe and were trying to work south straggled into the Rangers' positions from the seaward side and were killed or captured. Patrols rounded up other scattered enemy groups.

Of all the static positions, Sergeant Petty's outpost saw the most action, including rounding up a group of Poles conscripted into the German army who took the first opportunity to surrender. Some forty prisoners of war were taken in this way and held under guard in the field near the forward CP bunker.

Mid-afternoon Sergeant Lomell was in his fox-hole, a part of the coastal road-block, and saw an enemy force of about fifty troops moving tactically through the orchard to the north of the road. According to Lomell they had scouts out, two machine-gun teams and a 60mm mortar. They had approached so close obscured by the orchard that there was no time to react or even warn the twenty Rangers of Company D scattered along 150 yards of road. 'Lomell could only hope that the

Sergeant Lomell.

179

enemy would pass by and that his own men would have the sense to hold their fire.' The Germans, however, on approaching to within 10 yards of the road did not spot the Rangers and turned westward, moving parallel to the road before crossing it and heading south. Fire discipline among Company D had saved them from what could have been an extremely uncomfortable situation.

As night approached, the forward position was too thinly spread for safety and with the threat clearly coming from the south and west, Company D was pulled back from its more isolated position up by the road to a westerly-facing hedgerow. Company F on the other flank shortened their line, while Lieutenant Parker's men were used to thicken up the defences in small groups where required. Even so, it was a very thin line and walking along it today is to wonder why the five lieutenants forward did not withdraw to more defensible positions along the road.

The Germans had been assembling a substantial force during the evening, consisting of 12 *Kompanie* III/726 *Grenadier-Regiment* from Grandcamp, I/914 from Osmanville and apparently elements of II/916 who had been deployed inland to OMAHA Beach.

Around dusk Company D had reported seeing Germans in number to the south-west and so it was that the first attack south of the coastal road was launched by the Germans from that direction shortly after darkness had settled on D-Day at 2330 hours. It fell on the junction of Companies D and E, who were 'startled by a general outburst of whistles and shouts, close by on the orchard slope.' The

German troops on the march.

enemy opened a heavy fire including from a machine gun in front of Company D. This gun and its muzzle flashes were only 25 yards from their closest positions. Meanwhile in the darkness Company E spotted another machine gun about 50 yards from their defensive line. Nothing had been seen or heard of the stealthy enemy approach through the orchard. Elsewhere the enemy was almost on top of the Rangers as they began their final rush. In most cases, with the enemy silhouetted against the night sky the Rangers got the first shot off but none the less there were casualties that the Rangers could ill afford. The Germans had employed an Eastern Front tactic of crawling on their bellies to within easy assaulting distance with their own machine guns firing just over their head. The 'whistles and shouts' were designed to further distract the Rangers.

The official account records that 'Only a few minutes after the firing began, an immense sheet of flame shot up over to the west, near the position of the abandoned German guns.' This was probably further charge bags being set off by tracer rounds. 'The orchard slopes were fully lit up, and many Germans could be seen outlined against the glare. The flare died almost at once, and the firing ended at the same time.' Perhaps the powder explosion had disrupted the attack but more probably it was only a probing attack to draw the Rangers' fire and locate their positions.

With the attack having been beaten off, Sergeant Petty and his group of Company F men came under fire from the west and as a result withdrew successfully back up the hill to the main defensive line.

The next attack came from the south-west again but this time it overlapped further onto Company D's position. Starting at 0100 hours it began in the same way as before with a lot of shouting, which the Rangers speculated was designed to intimidate them with their numbers. This was followed by a considerable volume of fire that raked the hedgerows, with much of the tracer passing over the heads of the Rangers (the Eastern Front tactic again). The junction of the two companies was again the focus of the attack and this time the enemy crawled up close to the hedgerow and seized the corner before their attack ran out of steam. Gaining this toehold in the Rangers' position was a turning-point in the battle.

The assault was renewed at 0300 hours, probably in greater strength. With the Rangers running low on ammunition and with German supporting fire from the area of the corner, it had greater

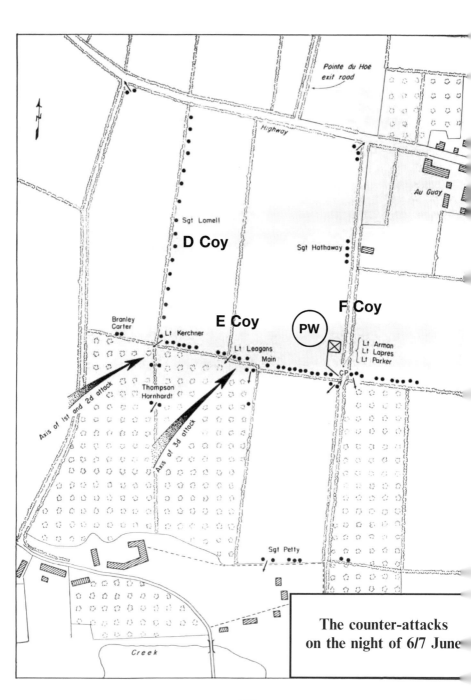

Pointe du Hoe exit road

Highway

Au Guay

Sgt Lomell

D Coy

Sgt Hathaway

E Coy

F Coy

PW

Branley
Carter

Lt Kerchner

Lt Leagans

Main

Lt Arman
Lt Lapres
Lt Parker

CP

Thompson
Hornhardt

Axis of 1st and 2d attack

Axis of 3d attack

Sgt Petty

**The counter-attacks
on the night of 6/7 June**

Creek

success. The third attack fell most heavily on Company E, whose positions on the northern side of the hedge were enfiladed from the corner.

It was an action that defies adequate explanation, as about twenty Rangers were taken prisoner, others were casualties and those who got back to Rudder had very different versions of events. The dark, made absolute by the loss of night vision from the flash of grenades, and misinterpreted noise are two of the problems inherent in night operations, but in this case they were compounded by the Rangers' use of German weapons and grenades.

What is plain is that the Germans were able to break into the western part of Company E's thirty-man line. The official report concludes:

> There is enough evidence to suggest that ... the main penetration now came near the middle of E's hedgerow and rolled up the Ranger positions west from there to the angle.
>
> One fox hole east of Lieutenant Leagans' post ... Pfc. Harold D. Main heard the Germans coming up close in the wheat just beyond the hedgerow. After a pause following the heavy opening fire, they rushed the hedgerow to Main's right, and Crook's BAR went silent. Minutes later, Main could hear Germans talking on his side of the hedge and knew what had happened. He crawled under the thick tangle of vines and briars into the middle of the hedgerow. Hidden there, he heard S/Sgt. Curtis A. Simmons surrender, only 15 feet away, but the Germans came no farther east.

Lieutenant Leagans was dead and Sergeant Rupinski and another group surrendered. Company E had been overrun. All that survived were individuals, lying low and missed by the Germans in the dark.

Lieutenant Parker's detachment with Company F came into action for the first time as the German attack extended east:

> A German party came eastward crossing the upper end of the wheat field; they were starting through the hedgerow embankment into the lane when Dix saw them only a few feet away from his post in the lane. He turned around to use the captured machine gun. It jammed on the first round, and a rifle bullet from some Ranger firing down the lane behind Dix hit a glancing blow on his helmet, stunning him. Recovering, and

starting to crawl along the hedgerow ditch back to the CP, Dix heard Petty yell 'Down!' just before opening with his BAR on Germans coming up the lane. Sergeant Robey's BAR joined in, and this fire broke up the only attack that came close to the CP. One German was caught crawling along the hedgerow into the CP area, and was killed by a grenade that landed directly under his chest. Plenty of fire was coming across the wheat field from the west, but no assault was tried from that quarter.

With a confused situation and incorrect information coming in to the forward CP, the decision was made by Lieutenant Arman to withdraw. In the case of the survivors of Company E this was under way already but the contingency of withdrawal had only been considered late and the plan had, in the prevailing circumstances, only been partly disseminated to the Ranger officers. The account of events on Company F's flank gives a flavour of the withdrawal:

As the volume of enemy fire built up again from south and west, indicating a new rush was at hand, hasty and informal measures were taken to pass the word around for withdrawal back to the highway and the Pointe. Some Rangers failed to get the notice and were temporarily left behind. Petty and Robey were told to bring up the rear and cover the withdrawal with their BARs. Non-commissioned officers tried hurriedly to round up their men. Once started, movement was fast. S/Sgt. Richard N. Hathaway of the 5th Rangers had been posted halfway back to the highway, along the lane. His first notice of what was happening came when men ran by toward the north. Hathaway stuck his head through the hedgerow and shouted 'Hey! What's up? Where you going?' The nearest man stopped running, put his rifle in Hathaway's face, and demanded the password. Hathaway was so rattled that he could just remember the word in time. Told 'the Germans are right behind us – get out quick to the Pointe!' he collected part of his group, and went north.

Browning Automatic Rifle (BAR).

Fortunately the Germans did not press their advantage and there was no pursuit north to the coast road. Some men, however, were missed, particularly Parker's men who had been inserted in the line without their normal chain of command and were left behind. Some of these men exfiltrated back to the Pointe, while others were added to the prisoners being mustered at the German battalion headquarters on La Montagne Road. However, about a dozen survivors of Company D, realizing what had happened, lay up in a well-covered ditch with the Germans moving around them.

In these circumstances, there was no option for the Rangers but to abandon the German prisoners who had been mostly taken earlier in the day, principally from the II/726 *Grenadier-Regiment*.

The I/914 *Grenadier-Regiment* had succeeded in driving the scant force of Rangers back in a five-hour battle. Some question Lieutenant Colonel Rudder's decision to maintain the position forward of the coast road but with the expectation of the 5th Battalion's imminent arrival this was an understandable risk. The difficulties of withdrawing at any point in contact with the enemy, and in the dark, speak for themselves.

Eventually by 0400 hours on 7 June, about fifty Rangers reached the defensive line at the Pointe and were inserted into the position,

Pointe du Hoc defence: D+1, 7 June.

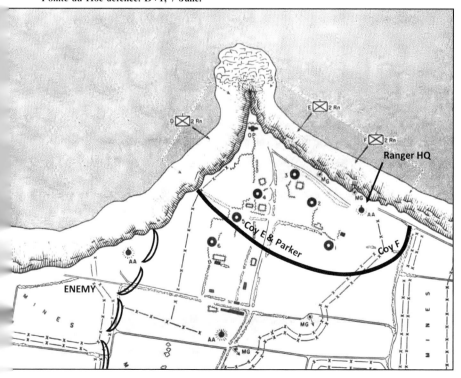

bringing Rudder's strength up to about ninety effectives but he had fifty seriously wounded to care for. The balance of nearly 250 men (including Parker's twenty-three) had either not made it to the Pointe, had been killed or were captured.

One Ranger commented 'I gave up hope of getting off Pointe du Hoc alive. No reinforcements in sight, plenty of Germans in front of us, nothing behind us but sheer cliffs and Channel ... We were up a creek not only for food and water but for ammunition.' The experienced Commando Lieutenant Colonel Trevor likewise remarked: 'Never have I been so convinced of anything as that I will be either a prisoner of war or a casualty by morning.'

7 June 1944: D+1

Dawn revealed that the Germans were in strength around them and the volume of artillery and mortar fire increased significantly. The natural conclusion was that they were preparing to attack and finish them off. With no word of relief Lieutenant Parker and seven of his men were tasked to make their way along the beach at the foot of the cliff (it was low water around dawn) to OMAHA and make commanders aware of the situation at Pointe du Hoc as quickly as possible.

The western anti-aircraft gun remained in enemy hands and occasionally in action throughout 7 June.

The D+1 reinforcement.

Lieutenant Parker being congratulated by Lieutenant Colonel Schneider after the battle.

Wounded Rangers from Pointe du Hoc evacuated to USS *Texas*.

With daylight, however, effective naval gunfire was able to resume, breaking up concentrations of German troops who looked as if they might be preparing an assault on the defence line.

With the situation easing at OMAHA Beach, the Ranger liaison officer aboard the headquarters ship was finally able to persuade commanders to send succour to Pointe du Hoc. Two LCVPs were dispatched under Major Street crammed with combat supplies and a platoon of twenty-four Rangers of the 5th Battalion who had originally been landed at the eastern end of OMAHA.

The redoubtable Lieutenant Parker delivered his situation report to OMAHA and set out to return with an outline of the V US Corps plan. Once again, he infiltrated through the German lines and the battery's wire and minefield to deliver his message. Rudder grunted and said: 'You men look hungry. We have plenty of bread, jam and spam. Go to it.'

Meanwhile, the 5th Battalion was marching to the relief of Pointe du Hoc and had already distracted the I/914 *Grenadier-Regiment* from attacking Rudder's hard-pressed force.

Chapter Nine

The Relief Column

Lieutenant Colonel Schneider and Ranger Force C consisting of his 5th Battalion and the remnants of 2nd Battalion's Companies A, B and C had been held back in defence of the western flank of the precarious OMAHA Beachhead on the evening of D-Day. Colonel Canham, with the support of his superiors, 'steadfastly refused to budge on the issue that evening.' Consequently, the Rangers dug in and patrolled out in front of their position.

Overnight Colonel Canham, with his battalion commanders, Schneider and an officer from the eight Shermans of C Company, 743rd Tank Battalion, who had reached Vierville at 2200 hours, planned the relief of Pointe du Hoc. At this stage, however, it was 'when circumstances allowed' but overnight a slackening of German pressure and insistence on mounting the operation by Schneider told and they were authorized to 'give it a go'.

At 0730 hours, the leading elements of the relief force were ready. The advance was to be spearheaded by a composite company of the 2nd Rangers under command of Captain Arnold followed by the depleted ranks of the 116th Infantry with Company C leading and several tanks. The advance guard had just disappeared out of sight to the west when, as feared, the enemy attacked Vierville from the south. Captain Raaen, Headquarter Company commander of the 5th Rangers, who had yet to move west, recalled:

Colonel Canham, 116th US Infantry Regiment.

> For me, D+1 started with a bang. The Germans attacked from the south with what seemed to be company strength. With the help of the 743rd Tank Battalion, parked on the main east-west road through Vierville, we held them off. The tanks had come up during the night, and this fight was the first I had seen of them. The tank crews were all buttoned up and could not

190

see or hear that we were being attacked. I jumped up on the hull of one and banged my rifle butt on the turret until a tanker opened his hatch. I then pointed out the attack and suggested he take the enemy under fire. He and the other tanks did just this, but only fired their .50 caliber machine guns, apparently believing that the targets were too undefined for them to use their 75mm cannons.

This attack was probably by elements of II/726 *Grenadier-Regiment* in support of a larger planned endeavour by the newly-arrived *Schnellbrigade* 30 against the beachhead further east. Once it had been beaten off, clearance patrols were dispatched to the south and west but little evidence of a renewed German attack was to be found.

The German attack being dealt with, Colonel Canham's main force, his 2nd and 3rd battalions along with the 5th Rangers, started to move west but they were low on ammunition of all types.

Meanwhile, with a bit of self-help (an abandoned Jeep), the 5th Rangers Headquarter Company, who had amid the chaotic aftermath of battle on the beach failed to secure a resupply the previous evening, now had plenty of that essential for a successful infantry advance into enemy territory – small-arms ammunition – to distribute to the companies.

Up ahead, using the D514 as their axis of advance, the scouts of the 2nd Rangers were in action. There were plenty of enemy troops

D+1 relief operations.

around but few were substantial organized bodies. The Rangers' methodology was when engaged to return fire and attempt to move on, leaving the tanks, that were following behind and safe from ambush amid the hedgerows, to 'brass-up' any stiff resistance. The necessary mopping-up was carried out by the following infantry. In this manner the relief force advanced over 3 miles, cutting through often stunned and surprised Germans. Colonel Canham's force was, however, strung out along the D514 with most of the 5th Rangers in the rear only just east of Vierville.

At 1100 hours the advance guard had passed through St Pierre-du-Mont and were just 1 mile east of Pointe du Hoc when they were halted by a large 15ft-deep crater in the centre of the road that blocked it, and what is more there was no apparent simple way around it for the tanks due to the number of marked minefields in the area. This crater, like the one in the marshy road behind GOLD Beach, could only have been caused by either a substantial Allied shell or bomb and also disrupted operations considerably.

None the less, being so close to the Pointe the composite company continued the advance but had only covered a matter of hundreds of yards before they were halted by machine-gun fire from Au Guay. The scouts were pinned down and it took fire and manoeuvre by Sergeant White's section to extricate the scouts and

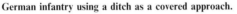

German infantry using a ditch as a covered approach.

occupy Au Guay. They had now reached the point where during the previous afternoon a BAR team from their Company F had been positioned 200 yards from the road down to the battery and the Pointe.

I/914 *Grenadier-Regiment* must have been unaware of the approach of the advance guard because their response was now both prompt and violent. Mortars and artillery as heavy as 150mm crashed down on the road from Au Guay to St Pierre-du-Mont. In expectation of counter-attack and with only four tanks beyond the shell-hole, the remainder of Company C motored into defensive positions.

Even though some tanks had got past the shell-hole, the methodology that had worked so well hitherto, relying on momentum, firepower and not too much opposition, had now broken down. With Company C of the 116th coming forward to Au Guay to deploy around the forward tanks, the weight of enemy fire redoubled; tanks were damaged and infantrymen were wounded. Both Rangers and infantry fell back to St Pierre in disorder. Captain Raaen was at the shell-hole:

> While I was there on the south edge of the crater, heavy artillery began falling perhaps 200 yards in front of me. A few moments later infantry began streaming by me through the crater.
>
> I saw that many were Rangers and used many a choice word on them. I was standing on the rim and the troops were in the crater below me. The fire that had driven them back did not come close so there was nothing to drive them on but panic, which subdued and they became more orderly.

At this point events at the OMAHA Beachhead intervened. The counter-attacks by the 352nd Division and *Schnellebrigade* 30 were causing concern, consequently both the tanks and most of the 116th Infantry were withdrawn, leaving the Composite Ranger Company, two companies of the 5th Rangers and C Company of the 116th to adopt a defensive position around St Pierre-du-Mont. Captain Raaen was in command, with the remainder of Headquarters Ranger Force C and two companies holding Vierville.

The Second Night

An afternoon of rumour and counter-rumour was broken by the first positive news that Rudder and his men were alive and holding

Rudder's command post. The US flag was displayed to prevent friendly aircraft firing at them and the bandaged head of Lieutenant Colonel Trevor.

out on the Pointe when Captain Raaen requested naval gunfire on supposed targets only to be told 'That's where your boys are!' About this time Lieutenant Colonels Schneider and Rudder were finally able to speak over an intermittent radio connection, with the latter requesting 'relief tonight'. With the enemy in battalion strength between the Pointe and St Pierre he was told that 'it will not be possible.' Rudder replied that he would be able to hold out until the following day. In the event there was no repetition of the major attacks of the previous night but the Germans were most definitely still active around the Pointe.

Physical contact between the two forces was, however, made between the two forces during the night of D+1/D+2. Firstly, the group of the 5th Rangers who had been landed at the Pointe that afternoon was sent out to make contact with the rest of their battalion, who it was known from the sound of battle must be close. They succeeded in slipping out via the eastern flank, avoiding

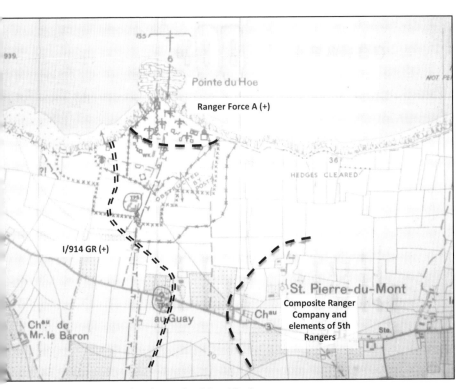

Pointe du Hoc: the situation on the night of D+1.

Germans moving around in the dark and crossing no man's land to St Pierre, with details of Ranger Force A's defensive line at the Pointe. Secondly, a pair of Rangers, Moody and McKissick, made a similar journey in the opposite direction; they went too far west in the dark but eventually reached Rudder's command post and passed their message detailing the situation in St Pierre and intentions. They returned to St Pierre and with a line-laying party of the 2nd Rangers' signallers paying out a telephone cable, direct and workable communications had at last been established. Both Moody and McKissick were awarded the DSC for a very dangerous operation during which they repeatedly crossed enemy territory and, almost as dangerously, entered friendly positions that were in close contact with the enemy.

D+2: Relief

Lieutenant Colonel Schneider returned to St Pierre arriving shortly after dawn, with the rest of his battalion following along with the 116th Infantry and the tanks of the 743rd Battalion. He was able to speak to Rudder by phone and tell him that the relief force would approach from the south-east, south and the south-west.

The Composite Ranger Company and D of the 5th Battalion were to be led by the cable-layers of the night before heading directly across from St Pierre to the Pointe, while the tanks escorted by elements of the 3rd 116th Infantry and a further two companies of the 5th Battalion would head south and then west, with the tanks and infantry escort then heading north up the tracks through the abandoned forward position. The two companies of Rangers would approach the battery from the west, while the 1st 116th Infantry would loop around further west. H-hour was at 0900 hours.

As the moves began, the destroyer USS *Ellyson* added to the fire plan engaging the German positions to the west of the Pointe with 140 rounds.

The operation started well but there was little effective synchronization, with the inevitable results. The composite company, however, led by its guides, walked straight into Rudder's defensive line from the east and were soon being greeted by the relieved Rangers, of which almost 40 per cent were now from the 5th Rangers. The tanks, taking the longer route to the south, reached the two forward lanes brushing aside minor opposition and turned north up the lanes towards the coastal road and battery.

The after-action report of Company C of the 743rd Tank Battalion records 'Attacked towards Pointe du Hoc (586937) at

Plan for the relief of Pointe du Hoc.

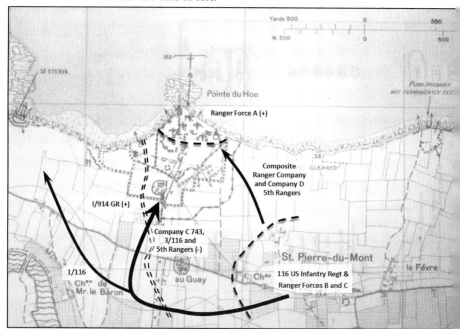

Relief members of the 2nd and 5th Rangers mingle amid the ruins of the battery.

1015 hours. Five tanks dropped out here. Five tanks hit mines and developed engine trouble. Four tanks were repairable.' As the Shermans of Company C advanced towards the already relieved battery the inevitable fratricide happened. Captain Raaen had already entered the battery from the east:

> By mid-morning 1000 hours, we had relieved the 2nd Rangers and were sitting around on the rubble of the gun position swapping our stories when all of a sudden, tanks of the 743rd Tank Battalion burst out of a patch of wood directly to our south and attacked us with machine-gun and cannon fire. A lieutenant of the 2nd Rangers ran out of cover, jumped up on one of the tanks, beat on the turret until he got the attention of the crew, put his pistol to the head of the tank commander . . .

Meanwhile Lieutenant Eikner, still in the CP, was now monitoring the common radio nets that had been established and shouted into his radio's microphone: 'Desist, desist. Stop firing.' Sad to say, there were fatalities and injuries because of this ill-coordinated action.

197

A German prisoner and sundry forced labour including Italian soldiers.

On a route even further west, the 5th Battalion Company was approaching. It is recorded that the western anti-aircraft casemate that had been in action on and off since D-Day and a haven for sniping at the Rangers' defence line around the Pointe surrendered. It is probable that they had little option now with tanks in front of them and a Ranger company closing in from behind!

The action at Pointe du Hoc was over and has forever gone down in the annals of American military history as one of its 'epics'. The cost, however, had been high. The landing strength of the Ranger battalions was around 450 men of which the 2nd Rangers, including Ranger Force B, lost 77 men killed in action, 152 wounded and 38 missing, most of whom it subsequently transpired were taken prisoner. The 5th Battalion, fighting a more conventional battle and during their landing benefiting from the experience of Lieutenant Colonel Schneider, avoided significant casualties on the beach and subsequently paying lower price of 20 killed, 51 wounded and 2 missing.

Casualties were evacuated in a variety of the 116th Infantry's transport and Jeep ambulances to a field hospital that had been

Officers of USS *Texas* visiting the battery after the battle to view their handiwork.

Another post-battle visitor on 12 June: General Eisenhower inspects the Pointe du Hoc guns with the Rangers who put them out of action.

established in Vierville but Rudder, despite his sundry wounds, remained with his Rangers.

Despite their experiences of the previous three days, after they had been fed, watered and otherwise re-equipped, the Rangers donned their fighting order, hefted their weapons and prepared to move. At 1600 hours the 2nd Ranger Battalion, now at little more than 50 per cent strength, marched south down the road and turned right to follow the 5th Battalion towards Grandcamp where they would rest. The battle had already moved on from Pointe du Hoc.

Chapter Ten

Subsequent Operations

The plan for D+2 on the western flank of the OMAHA Beachhead did not of course just focus on the relief of Pointe du Hoc. At the operational level, a link-up with the airborne troops and VIII US Corps (UTAH) the other side of the Vire estuary had still not been made but the Germans were now falling back and still resisting. US troops and equipment were pouring ashore across the beaches. The 29th Division's after-action report summarizes their orders for the day:

> D+2: 8 JUNE 1944. 29th Inf Div was ordered to continue the advance west to capture ISIGNY. The 115th Inf, with one company of 743rd Tank Bn attached, was ordered to seize and hold the LONGUEVLLE-NORMANVILLE ridge. The 116th Inf, (Atchd: 2nd and 5th Ranger Bns, 743rd Tank Bn less one Co, and one Co of 81st Cml Bn) was ordered to advance along coastal road, VIERVILLE-SUR-MER – GRANDCAMP – ISIGNY (excl.), to mop up enemy resistance in zone along the coast, and to protect the right flank of the 175th Inf. 175th Inf (atchd: 747th Tank Bn less one Co, one btry of 58th Armd FA Bn), was to continue its mission of advancing on ISIGNY. The Div Arty, less combat Team attachments, was ordered to coordinate naval and air support. IX AAF [Army Air Force] was to bomb ISIGNY with incendiary bombs prior to the attack of the 175th Inf.

See map on p. 202

Colonel Canham's part in this was with the 116th US Infantry, the Provisional Ranger Group and two companies of the 743rd Tank Battalion to protect the 175th Infantry's drive on Isigny. His tactical mission was to clear those German coastal strongpoints that were still occupied including those west of Grandcamp, plus several artillery batteries including those south of Maisy.

The Maisy Battery

There was no secret about the Maisy Battery at the time or since. It is clearly marked on the maps and features in the Provisional Ranger Group orders. There was no post-war attempt to hide its presence; like virtually every other battery, the French landowners

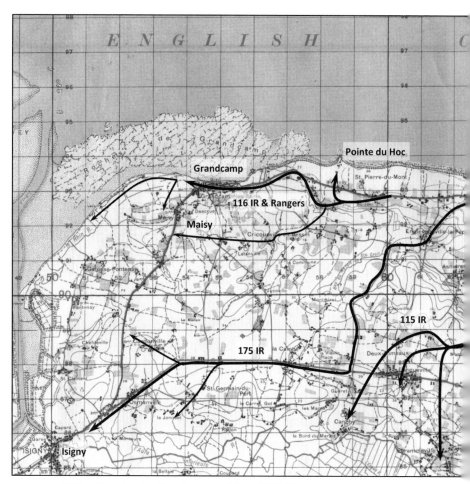

D+2 outline plans for the advance west from OMAHA.

simply filled in the trenches and resumed agriculture, leaving just the larger indestructible edifices standing above ground level. The three casemates above ground have been marked on French IGN maps as *Anc. Blockh.* [ancient blockhouse] since the 1960s! In the focus on the big story of D-Day many peripheral and/or subsequent actions have simply been 'forgotten'. The Rangers' action at the Maisy Battery on 9 June (D+3) is one such but information about it has been in the public domain in institutions and collections outside closed government archives in the form of maps and reports since the war.

As with the whole of the invasion coast, the Allied aircraft of the photo reconnaissance squadrons monitored Rommel's work to thicken up the Atlantic Wall and observed the development of the two adjacent batteries known as Maisy I and II to the Allies and as Wn 83 and 84 by the Germans. The air photo interpreters at the time assessed Maisy I as consisting of four 155mm (SFH 414 -f-) howitzers and Maisy II guns as being four 77mm field pieces of First World War vintage. On D-Day Wn 84 had three substantially-completed H699 casemates facing towards UTAH Beach covering the Vire estuary. The guns were crewed by the 8th and 9th Batteries of *Artillerie-Regiment* 1716. There was a third artillery position nearby, probably 155mm guns manned by the 10th Battery and known to the Americans as (naval) Target 180. There is, however, an unresolved debate about which units were manning which guns on D-Day. *Generalleutnant* Kraiss and his staff, of course, recast plans when the 352nd Division came forward to the coast and a significant number of companies were moved in accordance with his own tactical estimate and the increased number of troops available.

Like many of the other batteries, including the powerful 150mm naval battery at Longues-sur-Mer which could target shipping off both OMAHA and GOLD Beaches, the Maisy Battery was to be

The Maisy Battery as shown on the 20 May edition of the Defences Overprint map.

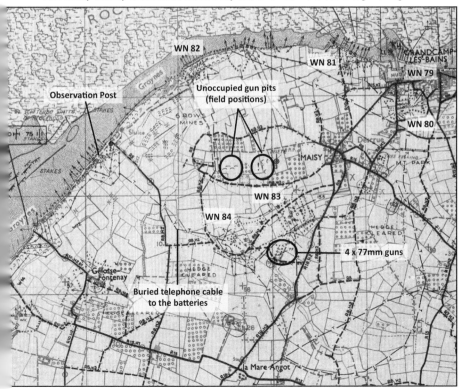

neutralized by the Navy until captured, as planned, late on D-Day or early on D+1. They were also the target on the night of 5/6 June of Free French heavy bombers operating alongside the RAF and during the preliminary pre-H-hour bombing by B-26 Marauder aircraft. This latter bombing as elsewhere was not very effective because of the weather conditions and poor light. As, however, can be seen from the extract from the Western Task Force's target list, both batteries at Maisy (T5 and T16) feature in the top five for the attention of the Bombardment Force.

On D-Day, following a bombardment by HMS *Hawkins*, the 155s at Maisy came into action against the fleet out to sea. The two ships nearest the batteries were the destroyers USS *Shubrick* and *Herndon*, both of which were initially firing in support of troops landing on UTAH Beach. Seaman Don Derrah was working as a part of *Shubrick*'s fire-control team and recorded that around

11thPHIB/A4-3(l) (a)
Serial: 00681

TOP SECRET — NEPTUNE

WESTERN NAVAL TASK FORCE
ASSAULT FORCE "0"
(TASK FORCE ONE TWO FOUR)
U.S.S. ANCON, Flagship
PORTLAND, DORSET.
20 May 1944; 1200.

APPENDIX 2
TO ANNEX F
GUNFIRE SUPPORT PLAN

LIST OF TARGETS

TARGET NO.	COORDIN- ATES	DESCRIPTION
T1	58609390	6 Guns, 155 mm
T5	53309180	4 Guns, 155 mm, 5 concrete shelters, 3 MGs, 1 Hut
T10	79268316	4 Guns, 105 mm
T16	52159150	4 Guns, 75 mm, 2 MGs, 1 Pillbox, 3 Shelters
T20	77008600	Strongpoint with possible 75 cal Guns
T21	76708775	7 MGs, 1 Pillbox
T22	76008780	2 MGs, 1 Hut, 1 Shelter
T23	75808785	4 MGs, 1 AT Gun
T24	75508790	1 Pillbox
T25	75308795	1 Pillbox. 1 MG
T26	75308838	1 Pillbox
T27	75008805	1 4.7 Gun, 3AA Guns. 6 Pillboxes
T28	75008790	5 MGs. 3 Shelters
T29	74908710	9 MGs, Road block. Troops in houses
T30	74508815	Strongpoint, 2 Arty Guns 2 Shelters

Task Force O gunfire support plan.

USS *Shubrick*.

Seaman Don Derrah.

0700 hours they were about 4,000 yards off Grandcamp and its German observation post in the church tower when

> shells from a battery (150mm) east of us are landing about 1,000 yards off our port beam (toward the beach) ... The shells on our starboard beam are getting closer. A splash every five minutes are its only indication. We couldn't seem to locate the gun.
>
> We have finally spotted a flash which we believe is from the battery that is after us. We just get on him – set up the problem and WHAM! We opened up rapid fire ... He has our range now and is getting pretty close. The Old Man ordered full speed astern in an attempt to fool him until our fire is effective. Our lookouts counted the splashes near us and judge that there are about eleven guns that are firing at us. It isn't more than a minute before our burst covers the area and begins taking effect. Both of us are putting out a lot of fire after six or seven more salvos and we cease firing to let the smoke and debris clear away. When it cleared they started to fire again, so did we, and that was all.

The navy's confidence in being able to neutralize enemy coastal artillery on D-Day was clearly justified.

D+2: The Advance from St Pierre-du-Mont

While four companies of Rangers, the 3rd Battalion, 116th US Infantry and some of the 743rd Tank Battalion's Shermans were relieving Ranger Force A at Pointe du Hoc, Colonel Canham's main force, along with Companies B and E of the 5th Rangers and the majority of the tanks were to advance west. Just over a mile beyond Pointe du Hoc movement was constricted by a substantial inundation and blocked by the Wn 78 strong-point. Setting off after the relief force sometime after 0900 hours, the two Ranger companies took the lead taking a southerly route via Château de M. Le Baron and along the northern edge of the inundation. Their mission was to secure the slightly higher ground on the outskirts of Grandcamp to the west of the sluice gate and Wn 78. By 1000 hours, with the advance led by Company B having gone well, the Rangers were approaching the bridge over the neck of the inundation and all was quiet ahead in Grandcamp.

Just 25 yards from the bridge with the leading Rangers out in the open, the enemy opened fire with machine guns and mortars

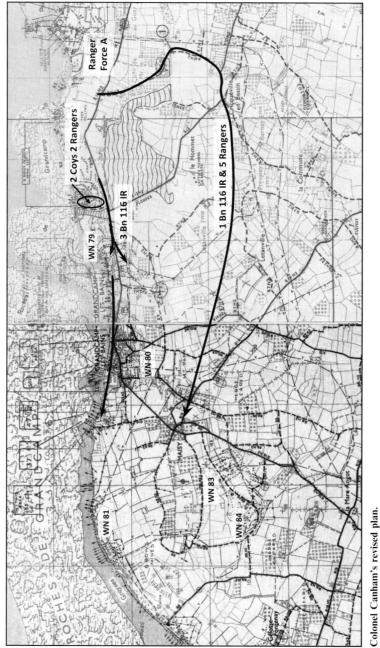

Colonel Canham's revised plan.

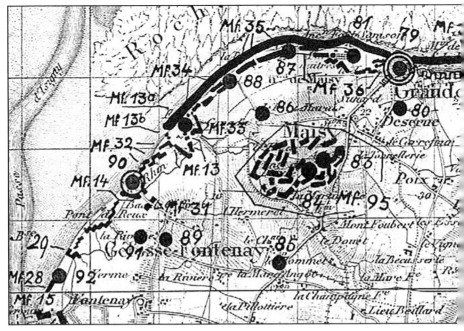

German minefields and defences in the Grandcamp area.

from the area of Wn 79 and pinned down Company B. Company C deployed to support and with fire and manoeuvre, including the use of smoke, B was extracted and joined C on the high ground east of the sluice gate. No. 914 *Grenadier-Regiment* and 12 *Kompanie*, 726 *Grenadier-Regiment* were clearly still holding Grandcamp in strength.

There is no mention of a fight to capture Wn 78 in the accounts of either the 116th Infantry or the Rangers. Consequently it is thought that the enemy abandoned the position, which was isolated by the inundation, in favour of strengthening the defences of Grandcamp (Wn 79).

Colonel Canham left the Rangers on their hillside from where they could both observe Grandcamp and give covering fire. He gave orders for the 1st Battalion, 116th Infantry, who had finished their clearance of the area immediately west of Pointe du Hoc, and also the three Ranger companies A, C and F who had been involved in the relief, to advance on the Maisy area. They were to head south around the inundation via Cricqueville-en-Bessin and then west towards Maisy. The remainder of the regiment and the tanks would force their way over the neck of the inundation and into Grandcamp. Company C of the 743rd Tank Battalion, which had earlier lost five tanks to mines at Pointe du Hoc, recorded: 'Advanced on Grandcamp-les-Bains (545931) at 1230 hrs. One more tank disabled due to mines.' The tanks of Company A that were following C explained in their after-action report: 'Moved on towards Grandcamp and because of mines on bridge reversed column.' With no way through for the tanks, they turned their Shermans around and Colonel Canham ordered Company A to join the move to Maisy via Cricqueville.

The Battle for Grandcamp-les-Bains

It took some time to coordinate the attack that was to be launched by the 3rd Battalion, 116th Infantry and the Shermans of C Company, 743rd Tank Battalion. In the meantime, the cruiser HMS *Glasgow* fired on the German strongpoints around Grandcamp, expending 113 rounds in 'softening-up the enemy' between 1455 and 1600 hours. *Glasgow* was the largest Allied ship firing on targets between Grandcamp and Isigny but certainly not the only one. The throw weight and fire effect of a single destroyer in an equivalent fire mission is said to match that of a battalion of 105mm guns on land.

The third battery of German field pieces to the south of the Maisy Battery complex was, according to the ship's log, engaged by USS *Shubrick* on 8 June 1944. Her log records that on 8 June she 'engaged a battery of German 150 mm (6in) field pieces, believed to be part of the Maisy Battery complex' and destroyed it.

The attack began with the tanks leading across the bridge, losing one vehicle in the process to a mine. Crossing the bridge and splashing through the inundation under cover of artillery fire that supressed the Germans sufficiently, Companies K and L of the 3rd Battalion 'worked over to the west bank'. Once across they attacked astride the road, Company K right and Company L left, with covering fire being provided by machine guns and BARs. The Official History records that 'Enemy emplacements north of the highway [Wn 79] had to be taken by close-in fighting ...' The citation for the Congressional Medal of Honor awarded to Technical Sergeant Frank Peregory of Company K provides a flavour of the action:

On 8 June 1944, 3rd Battalion, 116th Infantry was advancing on the strongly-held German defenses at Grandcamp-Maisy, France, when the leading elements were suddenly halted by

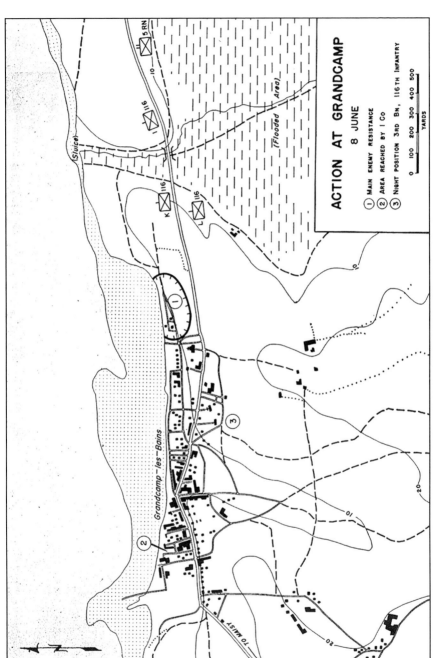

The attack on Grandcamp on 8 June 1944 from the US Official History.

decimating machine-gun fire from a firmly-entrenched enemy force on the high ground overlooking the town. After numerous attempts to neutralize the enemy position by supporting artillery and tank fire had proved ineffective, T/Sgt. Peregory, on his own initiative, advanced up the hill under withering fire, and worked his way to the crest where he discovered an entrenchment leading to the main enemy fortifications 200 yards away. Without hesitating, he leaped into the trench and moved toward the emplacement. Encountering a squad of enemy riflemen, he fearlessly attacked them with hand grenades and bayonet, killed eight and forced three to surrender. Continuing along the trench, he single-handedly forced the surrender of thirty-two more riflemen, captured the machine-gunners, and opened the way for the leading elements of the battalion to advance and secure its objective. The extraordinary gallantry and aggressiveness displayed by T/Sgt. Peregory are exemplary of the highest tradition of the armed forces.

Sadly, the award was made posthumously as Sergeant Peregory was killed in action six days later.

Meanwhile, Company L south of the road and under continuous small-arms fire broke into the outskirts of Grandcamp. Company I moved forward from reserve to clear the town in detail:

> ... snipers in the town continued to resist. Company I came up after the others had entered the town; one platoon of I, led by

The Congressional Medal of Honor.

Technical Sergeant Frank Peregory.

2nd Lt. Norvin Nathan, drove all the way through to the west end of Grandcamp and forced the surrender of a pillbox at the edge of the beach.

The tanks of Company A reported 'Position was taken at 1800 hrs' and that they were 'unable to continue on account of mines'. Organized resistance subsided and was over by dark and brought to a close an action which some soldiers of the 3rd Battalion, 116th Infantry described as more severe than their D-Day fighting.

Meanwhile, on the southern axis via Cricqueville the 1st Battalion, 116th Infantry, the Rangers and Shermans of Company A did not encounter enemy resistance until they were past the inundation and approaching the village of Maisy. Company A recorded that their Shermans 'Entered Maisy under mortar fire and machine gun fire, passed south out of Maisy on Isigny road. Enemy artillery and mortar fire was falling.' The official account records that: 'Heavy naval guns had torn Maisy to pieces, and the tanks were able to deal easily with resistance from enemy machine guns.'

The infantry followed on into the village to clear it but as the leading platoon of Shermans nosed beyond the houses they came under fire. Company A recorded that 'Two enemy pill boxes in strong point at 532915 were knocked out.' They had come up against the Maisy Battery:

Just west of the village an enemy strongpoint blocked the Isigny road and was supported by mortar and 88-mm fire, including interdictory fire behind Maisy which prevented reinforcement of the leading infantry elements. Since the tanks were running short of fuel, advance was halted for the night.

The 88mm guns reported were probably a part of *Flak-Abteilung* 266, which was redeployed to the Maisy area on D-Day with its dual-purpose anti-aircraft/anti-tank guns.

As darkness fell, the attack on both flanks ground to a halt. The infantry battalion remained in the villages holding their gains but as normal the tanks pulled back to leaguer for the night near the Ranger companies who had been in reserve.

The following diary extract from a US seaman demonstrates the often-overlooked battle that was continuing out to sea:

June 8: Underway for the assault area and sight France again at 1600. Boy, what a mass of ships. Three big groups close in, a

212

The dual-purpose 88mm gun.

line of destroyers extending as far as one can see, about ten miles out from the coast. This line is known as the Dixie line. It's primarily an E-boat screen. The sky wasn't exactly dark with planes, but there must have been two or three hundred bombers continuously overhead plus our screen of fighters. Shells from the larger shore batteries still are falling among the ships. We are in the inner screen, a few thousand yards from the transports. GQ [General Quarters] sounded at 2130 just before sunset. We had a very active night. Our advance screens have had constant contact with E-boats and are continuously putting up a barrage of star shells and service projectiles. We didn't do any firing but had to track all unidentified targets within 1500 yards. We had a BAKER WEST about midnight which means that enemy planes are in our vicinity. We can hear them make their runs and hear their bombs explode and the ships vibrate. Apparently, they're after the ships in the convoy. They're putting up a great deal of flack; one, perhaps two planes are shot down. The rest of the night is quiet. Two groups of enemy destroyers and E-boats were picked up about 12 miles out. Our outer screen drove them off. Word came over the TBS [tannoy] that the *Glennon* has hit a mine. She lost her fantail and gen. #4 [generator no. 4] and is floundering in the middle of a minefield now. Two LSTs [Landing Ship Tank]

213

were torpedoed while crossing the channel unescorted, last night. Had breakfast at GQ and only two hours of broken sleep since 0600 yesterday (June 8th).

The Maisy Battery: 9 June

During 8 June, the 29th Division's 175th Infantry had advanced as far as the outskirts of Isigny via La Cambe. This move threatened to cut off the I/914 *Grenadier-Regiment* in the increasingly narrow coastal strip between Grandcamp and Isigny. Consequently, *Generalleutnant* Kraiss ordered as many of his units as possible to escape through the bottleneck and to redeploy south of the River Aure where a new line was being established. In the event, during the short hours of summer darkness this withdrawal was very far from complete. The 352nd Division's command and control structure was breaking down and the confusion in the chain of command probably meant that some did not get the order and other static coastal units without transport were probably left to fend for themselves as best they could. The official US account of action north of the River Aure summarizes the German situation: 'At nightfall, the enemy forces still in this area were scattered and disorganized, and in one case prisoners accused their officers of

Prisoners of war included *Osttruppen* (eastern troops).

leaving the men to shift for themselves in an effort to get south and west of the Aure.'

Colonel Canham's orders for 9 June were to complete the clearance of the twenty *Widerstandsnest* in the coastal area south towards Isigny. This he elected to do with his own battalions leading, sending Lieutenant Colonel Schneider and the 5th Rangers' Companies B, D and E south via Le Manoir to Osmanville to protect his inland flank. This left Ranger Companies A, C and F as his reserve. B Company, 743rd Tank Battalion who had been in reserve back at Vierville for the previous few days, recorded that they 'Moved to Maisy (537923) where received orders to move South of Maisy.' The tank companies that had hitherto supported the 116th Infantry were allowed time for rest, replenishment and refit.

Advancing south-west from Grandcamp, the 116th Infantry almost immediately came under fire and encountered 'severe resistance' from the Maisy Battery. With 5 miles to clear down to Isigny and not wanting to get bogged down so close to his line of departure, Colonel Canham decided to bypass Maisy under cover of naval gunfire and leave it to Major Sullivan and his reserve companies of Rangers to deal with.

Local French civilians provided a great deal of assistance.

Seaman Don Derrah aboard the *Shubrick* recalled:

At dawn today (June 9th), the *Nevada* and the cruisers opened up, boom, boom, boom all day long ... GQ sounds ... as we move into our new station. We're going in to relieve another can [ship] 5,000 yards from the beach. Our purpose is to support the troops and knock out enemy strongpoints with the aid of a shore FC party. We are in 'restricted' waters, an area where only a few expendable ships are allowed because of the mines.

The Rangers were also supported by B Company, 81st Chemical Weapons Company (in the conventional role) with their 4.2in mortars and their own Company C's four 81mm mortars. In addition, attached from the 2nd Rangers, was pair of 75mm infantry cannons mounted on M3 White half-tracks. While an attack was being prepared, the batteries were engaged by the mortars and joined by the 105mm guns of the 58th Field Artillery Battalion. B Company recorded that their Shermans were called to deal with '... several pill boxes south of Maisy. 5th Rangers asked for support on these pill boxes, which were destroyed.'

With significant fire support the plan was to advance from Maisy village in column of companies in order F, A and C as reserve. As Company F moved forward out of the village towards their objective Wn 83 they came under fire from a hedgerow surrounding a small orchard to the south-west. They were halted and a desultory fire-fight resulted until the enemy was neutralized by indirect fire and the Rangers could move on. Meanwhile, Company A had followed out of the village and wheeled left to attack Wn 84.

Two problems confronted both of the Rangers' assault companies: mines and a marsh. Surrounding the Maisy Battery was an

Two 75mm cannon platoon vehicles supported the attack.

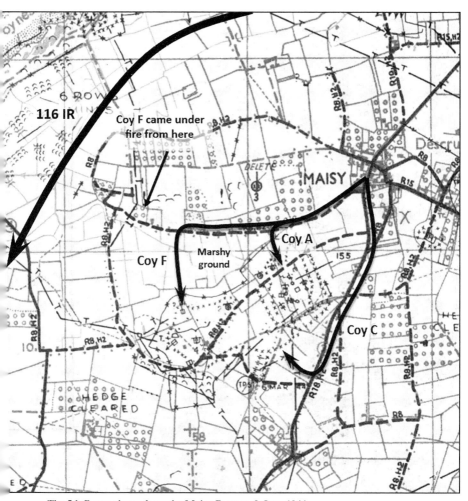

The 5th Rangers' attack on the Maisy Battery, 9 June 1944.

extensive minefield. Captain Raaen, who was following behind with his headquarters men, recalled:

> The mines outside the perimeter of the Maisy fortifications were orientated to block an attack from the north-west ... Most of the mines were 'Bouncing Bettys'. In the area where A Company would attack, these mines were connected in sets of about ten. When one mine of the ten was tripped the others would also detonate and that happened when Pfc John Bellows of A Company tripped a mine.

Several Rangers were wounded in this explosion.

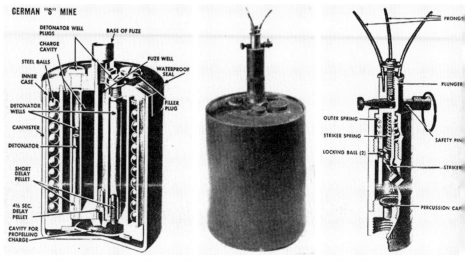

GERMAN "S" MINE

DETONATOR WELL PLUGS
CHARGE CAVITY
STEEL BALLS
INNER CASE
DETONATOR WELLS
CANNISTER
DETONATOR
SHORT DELAY PELLET
4½ SEC. DELAY PELLET
CAVITY FOR PROPELLING CHARGE

BASE OF FUZE
FUZE WELL
WATERPROOF SEAL
FILLER PLUG

PRONGS
PLUNGER
OUTER SPRING
STRIKER SPRING
LOCKING BALL (2)
SAFETY PIN
STRIKER
PERCUSSION CAP

German S-mines or *Schrapnellmine*, known to the Americans as 'Bouncing Betties'.

Both assault companies had to cross a broad marsh to reach the battery. Company A, hearing F in action at Wn 83, began their attack which literally bogged down in mud and water. Under fire the Rangers withdrew and redeployed a little further west where ground conditions were better and enemy fire less for a determined second attempt. As Company A pressed home their attack, resistance started to slacken. Lieutenant Parker recorded that German officers or NCOs were shooting their comrades who attempted to surrender. Understandably, 'From there on, the defence stiffened and nobody dared surrender.' Many of those who successfully surrendered were Poles. It was, however, slow going fighting through the battery position.

Meanwhile, Company F was attempting to break through the ring of mutually-supporting *Tobrukstand* machine-gun positions that surrounded Wn 83. After winning a fire-fight with small arms and with the enemy machine guns thus suppressed, Rangers crawled forward to within throwing range and were able to blow these positions with a mix of grenades and satchel charges. This broke the chain of overlapping and interlocking machine-gun arcs of fire that protected the battery. Private First Class Dan Farley recalled the fight in Wn 83:

> We got up there and it was all underground bunkers. We got in and started hand-to-hand combat. We finally got the walkway [covered trenches] and came out into the opening and then went into another one – one right after the other. It was

218

Tobrukstand **positions tended to be stand-alone bunkers on the edge of a battery, or if sited in the centre of a battery they were incorporated in other structures.**

completely dark in the tunnels. I got shot in the shoulder, I think by a sniper. Maisy Battery was just as bad as OMAHA Beach, if not worse!

With both attacks in danger of stalling, Major Sullivan deployed his reserve Company C and the two cannon platoon vehicles from the village down the road heading south. Wheeling to the right they joined the battle for Wn 83 with the two 75mm guns engaging targets but even so, it was slow work. Major Sullivan dismounted from the half-tracks to better control the battle and his Distinguished Service Cross (DSC) citation explains his role in getting the attack going again:

> In cooperation with United States Infantry an attack was begun on the ——— [Maisy] battery. When certain elements were temporarily halted by artillery fire Major Sullivan, who had been wounded at ——— [Maisy], calmly and courageously rallied his officers and men, ordered a renewal of the attack, and instead of bypassing the resistance, advanced over heavily-mined terrain to capture the ——— [Maisy] battery with a loss of only fifteen men.

The Distinguished Service Cross.

With Companies C and F converging head-on, it was inevitable that they would end up shooting at each other. Consequently, when this started to happen Major Sullivan, who had been slightly wounded in the minefield, withdrew Company C, which was reinserted attacking from the east; i.e. with a much safer 90-degree angle between attacking companies. Together they fought their way through the enemy positions. There were pockets of resistance fighting on alongside groups of Germans who clearly wanted to surrender, which made for a difficult fight for both attacker and defender alike. Private Gray recalled that after the battery '... had been captured, I do remember some German firing a gun after everyone had surrendered and someone took him out and shot him!'

During the action at the Maisy Battery that lasted into the early afternoon, eighteen Rangers became casualties.

The guns captured were not those expected. The Rangers' after-action report states that the three guns in the Wn 83 casemates were 105mm but whether they were original German guns or re-chambered and re-bored captured guns remains debatable, as is

Minefields around the Maisy Battery were numerous.

the type and quantity reported in Wn 84. The Royal Navy's Official History, based on a Combined Ops survey conducted in the weeks after D-Day, states Maisy Battery I (Wn 83) as having four 105mm guns and Maisy II Battery (Wn 84) a single 105mm. With so many variables and the changing of weapons along the front taken over by the 352nd Division when they came forward to thicken up the defences, identifying exactly which type of guns were at Maisy is probably impossible.

The 5th Rangers' after-action report and other accounts similarly also disagree on the number of prisoners taken during the capture of Maisy but figures of 20 dead and between 90, 125 and 169 prisoners are in the correct range within the battery area. Statements of 'hundreds' of prisoners can be accounted for by those who surrendered in the surrounding area and by those rounded up en route south to join the rest of the Provisional Ranger Group at Osmanville for a well-earned rest.

A Tour of Pointe du Hoc

Pointe du Hoc is located off a roundabout on the D514 coastal road approximately halfway between Grandcamp-Maisy and Vierville-OMAHA.

The address and other details are as follows:

Site de la Pointe du Hoc
14450 Cricqueville-en-Bessin
Long./Lat.: 49.3971886, –0.9892703

The site is managed by the American Battle Monuments Commission (ABMC) and is open daily, all year round, between 0900 and 1700 hours.

It is recommended that the visitor follows the path in an anti-clockwise direction via the visitor centre and commemorative area. This path takes in all the key features of the battery and scenes of the action described in the chapters of this book, although there is plenty more of Pointe du Hoc to be explored away from the made-up paths.

Pointe du Hoc visitor circuit.

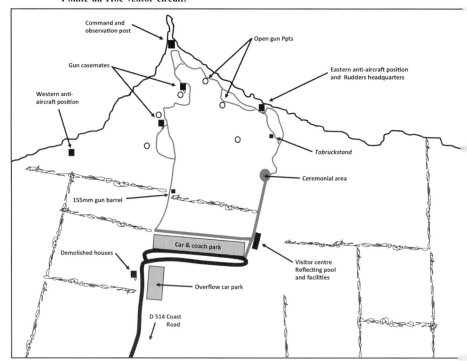

One of the *Tobrukstand* machine-gun positions and a near-miss shell-hole.

Rudder's HQ below the eastern anti-aircraft position.

One of the abandoned open gun-pits and the viewing platform on one of the casemates.

The viewing slit for the observation post's stereoscopic range-finder.

The 155mm gun barrel on display at Pointe du Hoc.

A Tour of the Inland Position

A visit to the battery of course covers only a part of the story of the Rangers at Pointe du Hoc and would not be complete without looking at the site of Sergeant Lomell's destruction of the guns and the counter-attacks on the night of D-Day.

Leave the battery via the access road, passing farm buildings on the right that Rangers cleared during their advance south. At the roundabout turn right onto the D514 towards Grandcamp. After 250 metres, there is a track to the left heading south (unsuitable for motor vehicles). This track is sometimes a little overgrown but leads to the site of the missing guns and crosses the axis of the German counter-attacks. Only vestiges of the orchards remain.

On reaching La Montagne Road turn left (east) and walk about 250 metres to a track junction on the left just short of a bridge. Take the right fork and follow.

The track runs up north towards Au Guay, bisects Company F's position and its withdrawal route.

On reaching the road in the hamlet of Au Guay, the visitor is at the furthest point reached by the 5th Rangers and Company C, 116th US Infantry on the afternoon of D+1.

Tour of the inland position.

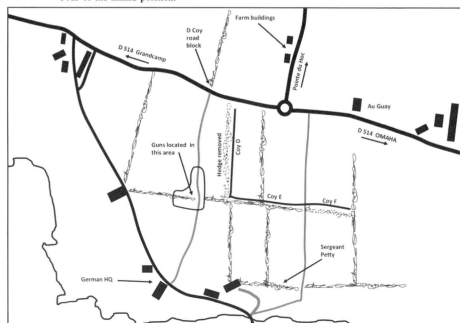

The junction on La Montagne Road and the view up towards Sergeant Petty's forward position.

Appendix III

A Visit to OMAHA Beach DOG Sector

A visit to OMAHA Beach is always impressive but timing a visit when the tide is out is best. Details of the state of the tides can be found online by searching 'tide times Grandcamp-Maisy'. It is, however, fortunate that a good view of the action is available from the beach and the Mulberry A pontoon as access to the bluffs behind DOG Sector is effectively precluded by the string of villas and a lack of rights of way, although a footpath (GR 223) runs across country several hundred yards inland from the top of the bluffs from Hamel au Prêtre to the Les Moulins draw.

From the D514 crossroads at Vierville take the D517 down the DOG 1 draw, passing the sections of floating roadway from the Mulberry harbours. They were recovered from isolated bridges across Normandy where they had been in use since they replaced the original Bailey bridging that was needed for the Rhine crossing.

Park in the large car park. Just across the pedestrian crossing is a small memorial to the 5th Rangers, while to the east above the houses are several 'murder holes', a part of Wn 71, covering the draw.

The large set of casemates that make up *Widerstandsnest* 72 block the foot of the draw. Looking west onto CHARLIE Sector and a little to the east it is easy to appreciate the gauntlet of fire that had to be run by the three companies of the 2nd Rangers to get to the modest cover available at the back of the beach.

Wn 73 up on the cliffs at the western end of OMAHA is accessible but overgrown. At the time of writing, however, the coastal path that bisects it is closed as the cliffs are unstable. It is consequently recommended that the signs are respected. Access is permitted up as far as the field gun casemate.

Having inspected the memorials around Wn 72, proceed east along the beach road. Stop 500 yards short of the memorials at the foot of the Les Moulins draw. This is more or less the centre of the 5th Rangers' landing and the bluffs up which they led the way into the gap between Wn 68 and Wn 70.

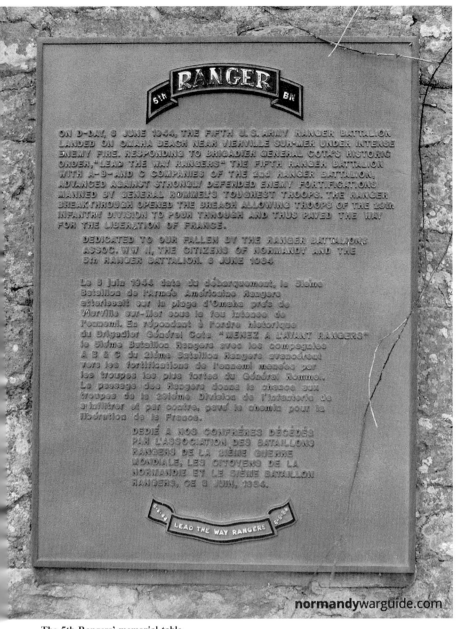

RANGER

5th BN

ON D-DAY, 6 JUNE 1944, THE FIFTH U.S. ARMY RANGER BATTALION LANDED ON OMAHA BEACH NEAR VIERVILLE SUR-MER UNDER INTENSE ENEMY FIRE. RESPONDING TO BRIGADIER GENERAL COTA'S HISTORIC ORDER, "LEAD THE WAY RANGERS" THE FIFTH RANGER BATTALION WITH A-B-AND C COMPANIES OF THE 2nd RANGER BATTALION, ADVANCED AGAINST STRONGLY DEFENDED ENEMY FORTIFICATIONS MANNED BY GENERAL ROMMEL'S TOUGHEST TROOPS. THE RANGER BREAKTHROUGH OPENED THE BREACH ALLOWING TROOPS OF THE 29th INFANTRY DIVISION TO POUR THROUGH AND THUS PAVED THE WAY FOR THE LIBERATION OF FRANCE.

DEDICATED TO OUR FALLEN BY THE RANGER BATTALIONS ASSOC. WW II, THE CITIZENS OF NORMANDY AND THE 5th RANGER BATTALION. 6 JUNE 1994

Le 6 juin 1944 date du débarquement, le 5ième Bataillon de l'Armée Américaine Rangers atterissait sur la plage d'Omaha près de Vierville sur-Mer sous le feu intense de l'ennemi. En répondant à l'ordre historique du Brigadier Général Cota "MENEZ A L'AVANT RANGERS" le 5ième Bataillon Rangers avec les compagnies A B & C du 2ième Bataillon Rangers avancèrent vers les fortifications de l'ennemi menées par les troupes les plus fortes du Général Rommel. Le passage des Rangers donna la chance aux troupes de la 29ième Division de l'Infanterie de s'infiltrer et par contre, pavé le chemin pour la libération de la France.

DEDIÉ A NOS CONFRÈRES DÉCÉDÉS PAR L'ASSOCIATION DES BATAILLONS RANGERS DE LA 2IÈME GUERRE MONDIALE, LES CITOYENS DE LA NORMANDIE ET LE 5IÈME BATAILLON RANGERS, CE 6 JUIN, 1994.

6-6-44 LEAD THE WAY RANGERS 6-6-94

normandywarguide.com

The 5th Rangers' memorial table.

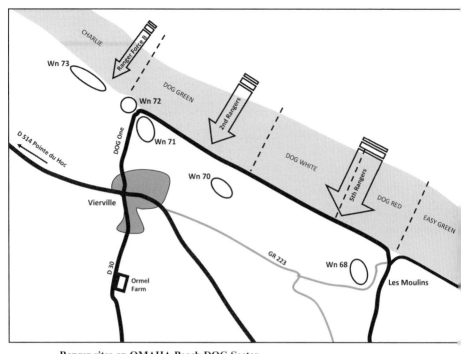

Ranger sites on OMAHA Beach DOG Sector.

The 'murder holes'.

The view from the Mulberry float across Wn 72 up to Wn 71.

Looking up from Wn 72 to Wn 73 and the cliffs to the west.

Index

232

234